MW00876203

The Virgin Mary and the Apostles of the Last Times (according to St. Louis-Marie de Montfort)

by

Fr. Antonin Lhoumeau, Montfort Father

Copyright © 2012 Casimir Valla

All rights reserved.

This book, in whole or in part, may not be reproduced or transmitted in any form or by any means, electronic or mechanical, including, but not limited to, audio recordings, facsimiles, photocopying, email, floppy disk, network, or information storage and retrieval systems without explicit written permission, dated and signed from the publisher.

"God wishes that His holy Mother should be at present more known, more loved, more honoured, than she has ever been" [St. Louis-Marie Grignion de Montfort, *Treatise on the True Devotion to Mary*, n° 55].

For more excellent Marian books, visit:

BlessedMaryMotherofGod.com

Table of Contents

Foreword

St. Louis-Marie de Montfort "wrote some spiritual treatises, which have already had a remarkable influence on the Church during the few years they have been known, and bid fair to have a much wider influence in years to come. His preaching, his writing, and his conversation were all impregnated with prophecy, and with anticipations of the latter ages of the Church. He comes forward, like another St. Vincent Ferrer, as if on the days bordering on the Last Judgment, and proclaims that he brings an authentic message from God about the greater honour and wider knowledge and more prominent love of His Blessed Mother, and her connexion with the second advent of her Son" [Fr. Faber, Preface from the English translation of *The True Devotion*].

These remarkable words testify that the great ascetical writer had understood well the importance and originality of the prophetic insights of our Saint. How many people since have read and even quoted the pages to which he alluded without fathoming the meaning of them, nor measuring the impact of them! The complement which God gives to the works of the saints – *et complevit labores illius* – consists as much in the development of their works as in that of their thoughts, which illuminate the sequel of events at the bidding of Providence. It is necessary to speak not only of exterior events, but also of the movement of the interior life of the Church, the progress in the knowledge of the mysteries and in devotion. We cannot doubt that in our days, and for these two reasons, that the life and writings of St. Louis-Marie de Montfort are better understood and that their influence increases tremendously. This progress will continue. From now on let us not shrink the prophetic insights of our Saint to the limits of a peculiarity of his writings that is original and interesting, but, somehow, purely episodic. These views alone make it possible to measure in all their scope the impact of the Marian teaching of Montfort, to make a synthesis of his devotions and of his spiritual life. Apart from them, the influence of his writings in the Church cannot be understood in the past nor be conjectured for the future.

A remarkable coincidence! Montfort had announced that in the divine plan the time would come when Mary would be even more glorified; and, as the glory of the Blessed Virgin grows, we see increasing also that of her servant. May this work bring to Mary many souls, especially priestly souls, who, giving themselves to her unreservedly, serve her according to the insights and desires of the one who sang:

I shall give my life
To win a heart for her.

(Hymn of St. Louis-Marie de Montfort)

Chapter I

The End Times

Numerous are the texts of Sacred Scripture in which this expression is found: *In novissimis diebus; in novissimo tempore*: In the last days, in the last time. This adjective *last* is relative; it can indicate a relation with what precedes, without always meaning that nothing more will follow. Christian language gives the name 'last times' to this period of an undoubtedly indeterminate duration, which can encompass years and centuries, but in which catastrophes, events of every kind, particularly the battles of the Church, her humiliations and triumphs, everything, finally, will have an extreme, and, so to speak, terminal, character which will prepare the second advent of Christ.

In the history of the world, the principal fact is the coming of the Son of God. The first time, He appeared to us in the infirmity of our human nature in order to redeem us; but He must return at the end of time in all the brilliance of His glory. This is what is called the *parousia*.

This return of Christ is the object of our faith; the Master Himself has ordered us to watch and wait. He will return for each of us at death; but there will be a second advent for everyone, when He must judge the world and close the course of the centuries. Its date remains the secret of God.

It is this last coming that is the question here. For those who know how to suffer and weep in this vale of tears, who hunger and thirst for justice and long for the kingdom of God, this coming will be a deliverance and an elation. According to the word of the Master, they will raise their head as a sign of their joy, for their redemption is at hand: "Lift up your heads, because your redemption is at hand" [Lk. 21:28]. We understand that the first Christians expected ardently, and with some impatience this coming of the beloved Master Whom several had seen in the days of His earthly life, and

Whose return had been promised to them by angels on the day of the Ascension, without fixing any date. Several times the Apostles had to speak of this second advent of Jesus; because it became necessary to support Christian faith and hope, by preserving minds from errors along various lines which tended to weaken them.

Time went by; the social condition of the Church had changed; and, as it says in the parable of the virgins, when the Spouse was late in coming, they fell asleep, no longer waited, and no longer kept watch. This phenomenon is found in periods of peace. The more we enjoy, the less we wait; and when evils diminish, the less we long for deliverance. Unhappy times come, catastrophes and upheavals, such as the ruin of Jerusalem and the dispersion of the Jews, the decline and fall of the Roman Empire, and the invasion of the barbarians. Then the thought of the second advent of Christ is awakened with fears of the end of the world. It preoccupied the better minds, such as St. Gregory the Great; it seized and shook the crowds, and it inspired poems and popular songs.

These considerations seem to make the mission of St. Louis-Marie de Montfort appear stranger, almost inconceivable. He was announced by St. Vincent Ferrer, and, like him, prophesied about the end times, but in a different light. The great century had just ended. Despite many calamities, minds were as settled in the midst of vanities of every kind and the pleasures of a refined civilization, far, very far from being concerned about the return of Christ. It is not that piety and the mystical life had disappeared in this period which furnished the Church her contingent of saints and incontestable glories; but Jansenism had, in the churches of France, a general and profound influence, which sharply contrasted with the apostolate of the Saint. He echoed St. John, when he showed the just of the earth longing for the coming of the Lord: and he asked for it, like St. Paul, in order to reestablish all things in order and justice: "Every creature groaneth and travaileth even till now" [Rom. 8:22].

Sighs of love in faithful souls are quite different from the servile fear that Jansenism preached, by only speaking of the coming of Jesus through terrors, without confidence in the last judgment. As for receiving Eucharistic Communion, according to the precept of St. Paul, in memory of Christ and in expectation of His return (*until He come* [1 Cor. 11:26]), heresy turned the faithful away from it. Montfort, on the contrary, invited them to it in tones of an ardent charity. With a hateful ruse inspired by satan, it worked also to diminish the Virgin Mary in the mind of Christians and to separate them from devotion to her. And it is in the depths of these thick shadows that Montfort cast his dazzling sermons and his inflamed and bold writings on all sides. Not content to proclaim the excellences of Mary in magnificent terms and to encourage devotion to her even to the point of holy slavery, he also opens vast perspectives on her role in the Church, particularly in the last ages in which she must prepare for the second coming of Jesus. "God wants to end the years of grace through Mary, as He began them through Her." Finally, to this world which is already agitated by the premonition of imminent upheavals, in which Christianity is attacked in every way, Montfort proclaims his *Fiery Prayer*, a true battle cry, a call to an ardent offensive against the enemies of God. He announces in it that he was attacking them with fire, the renewal of the earth, and the triumphs of the Church. At the summit of this strange, even inopportune contrast, it is to the world in love with the earth, its peace, and its happiness and which longs no more for the coming of Christ, that the Saint affirms that his prophetic insights will be realized "particularly at the end of the world *and soon*."

Did he make a mistake and commit an anachronism? His contemporaries could think so, and those who followed them perhaps did not sufficiently connect the events that had taken place to these prophetic words. The past and the present justify them completely; and we notice today how Montfort had reason to speak of the end times as being close. They were going to begin, even if they had not already commenced; because then were outlined the signs which in our days are emphasized more clearly and more universally.

These times, we said, are characterized by events which prepare, along with the end of the Church militant, the return of Christ in the glory of His triumph. Among these events or signs, several have been commonly admitted for a long time. The Catechism of the Council of Trent expressly indicates three: the preaching of the Gospel throughout world, the apostasy of the peoples, and the reign of Antichrist. The conversion of the Jews and other events which are connected to these signs by concomitance or consequence are manifested in our days. Finally, Saint Louis-Marie de Montfort has on this question some indications which are his own and which it is advisable to examine.

I

It is generally thought that the evangelization of the world is nearing its conclusion or little is lacking for it. In the 17th century, it was well advanced. The missions in Canada, for which Montfort burned to consecrate himself, were a great step in this evangelization of America. In the 19th century, this was principally Africa's turn. The progress of industry favors the penetration of Christianity in every country. Before long, aviation will undoubtedly open to missionaries routes to reach the depths of continents and the remotest islands. This preaching of the Gospel which Jesus gave to His apostles as a sign of His coming and of the consummation of the world is, then, on the way to complete realization. "*Et praedicabitur hoc evangelium regni in universo orbe, in testimonium omnibus gentibus; et tunc venient consummatio.*" "And this gospel of the kingdom, shall be preached in the whole world, for a testimony to all nations, and then shall the consummation come" [Mt. 24:14].

II

After the conversion to Christianity will come the dechristianization by loss of faith in individuals and by the apostasy of the nations. It is the second sign and we also read it in holy Scripture. "But yet the Son of man, when He cometh, shall He find, think you, faith on earth" [Lk. 18:8]? *Filius hominis veniens putas, inveniet fidem in terra*? St. Paul, speaking of the precursory signs of the Antichrist at the end of the world, mentions apostasy, separation from the Church of Christ, and desertion from the faith which have to precede the coming of the Lord. "For unless there come a revolt first" [2 Th. 2:3].

In the era when St. Louis-Marie de Montfort lived, this twofold work of dechristianization in nations was already begun. There were in every time crimes, disorders, impiety, and heresies, and the Middle Ages were not exempt from them. The satanic mysteries themselves had secret shelters there. But the disruption caused in the world by Luther was quite another thing. Personal interpretation ruined the faith, and the revolt against the Church her Head disrupted what was called Christendom. Philosophism, in the 18th century, put in fashion an elegant and derisive skepticism. Basically, the watchword came from hell against the Church, and soon persecution raged in Portugal, Josephism in Austria, and Jansenism and Gallicanism in France. Nations big and small had gone over into Protestantism. It was, then, the faithful summary of a very imminent future which our great missionary made when he exclaimed: "Your divine faith is transgressed, Your Gospel is abandoned; torrents of injustice flood the whole earth and lead astray even Your servants; the whole earth is desolate; impiety is enthroned; Your sanctuary is profaned and abomination is even in the holy place" (*Prayer*).

But, for two centuries, how the infernal work has progressed! The Revolution, satanic in its nature, upset the whole world by its ideas and deeds. The apostasy of the nations is virtually consummated, not only by heresy, but by the more radical idea of naturalism. The religious secularism of the State in all its institutions and in its manifestations in public life has become a fundamental and indisputable principle. Peoples are so profoundly imbued with this error, that the propositions of the *Syllabus*, which are conformed to right reason, collide with inflexible opposition; while the Declaration of the rights of man, so foolish in its composition, but so perverse in its spirit, finds acceptance by so many good souls. One may object that several nations are still Catholic by the religion of the State, and that the others at least make official religious acts. But heresy has become the religion of the State with the tolerance of Catholicism, or the freedom of worship which, in theory as in practice, puts on the same foot error and truth, is indeed apostasy. Now count the small number of officially Catholic nations. And even there, in spite of the religious acts of their public life, is it the interests of the Church, the defense of the faith or Christian morality which inspire their enterprises, their diplomacy, their declarations of war and their treatises of peace? No; it is the thirst for domination, the eagerness for gain, the safeguarding of purely material interests, elegantly named economic development. When these States give to God the alms of a place in their life, "it is," says one writer, "a way of annexing to their empire the former prestige of the King of kings."

If nations apostatize, will God at least find refuge in the conscience and in the soul of individuals? No; because it is there that satan wants to destroy the faith. Heresies attacked a particular truth; schism separated the branch from the trunk by cutting the tie of authority; but it is our time which sees the blossoming in the maturity of all its consequences this fruit of Lutheranism which has name Kantianism. It is faith itself; it is also natural reason which, in a frenzy of pride, it kills radically in order to deify the *self*. By means of this air pump, minds empty themselves from the inside of all dogma and all moral law; finally, modernism, under its varied forms, ravages souls and prepares for the domination and cult of satan; because that is where it all leads to. There is doubtless an elite which resists, and we also see conversions, but the masses lose the faith. Will there be a return, a reaction, which will have to result from some sort of prodigy? We hope so; but after this halt in the progress of evil, after this renewal worked by the Spirit of God, we can also guess a new offensive against the faith by seductions and threats: this will be the approach of the last calamities.

III

A third sign mentioned by the Catechism of the Council of Trent and which is also found in sacred Scripture is the reign of Antichrist, the son of perdition, rising up against everything which is called God or is adored, because divine [cf. 2 Th. 2]. Montfort seems to have understood the preparations for this final assault of hell against Christ and His Church, of these supreme battles. "The enemies of God," he said, "have already sounded the alarm: *Sonuerunt, frenduerunt, fremuerunt, multiplicati sunt.*" The great missionary was hardly lying in his grave when the synagogue of satan was formed in its modern organization: freemasonry. It celebrated its bicentenary in the year 1917, in coinciding with Luther's fourth centenary. It was the antichurch, grouping the forces of evil and, notwithstanding the diversity, and sometimes the opposition of their interests, uniting them in the same hatred of God and in war against His Christ. This association of ill-matched elements for the same purpose, whether it be of individuals or nations, Montfort denounces when he shows "the earth and the sea covered with an innumerable multitude of outcasts who, although all divided from one another, either by the distance of places, or by difference of disposition, or by their own interests, unite, however, all together till death, to wage war against You (O God) under the banner and direction of the devil" (Prayer). Behold international or universal masonry, the unity of its purpose for which it exploits even the variety of interests of the nations. Less than a century after the death of the Saint, it caused the French Revolution, methodically prepared and executed. It was a first attempt at the universal reign of satan, because it spread in Europe, and even beyond, its ideas and politics. Then, after a latent period of activity, Masonry pursued its anti-Christian work by the abasement of Catholic nations, the exaltation of peoples dedicated to Protestantism and by establishment of great national unities: Italian unity against the papacy, German unity against Austria and France, and others afoot. The Franco-German war in 1870 was a decisive period. Austria had already been annexed by Prussia since Sadowa. The defeat of France allowed the German States to be confederated in an empire whose power was imposed upon the world. Masonry had found in this new Caesar its soldier and instrument, as formerly Christ had found His sergeant in the king of France. By the Triple Alliance (such a bizarre alliance of the three States), Germany guaranteed to Italy the despoliation of the papacy and kept humiliated Austria on a leash. At the same time, it imposed on a conquered France religious persecution and the masonic republic, which had to lead it to official atheism and push it to the abyss. It was necessary, according to the word of Bismarck, to destroy France in order to overcome Catholicism more easily. And for forty years, helped by Masonry, Germany prepared with its triumph that of Lutheranism over the Catholic Church. Its empire over all the nations, which appeared more formidable than we had foreseen, was only able to take place so easily thanks to this universal assistance. This influence was not only in the economic domain, it happened in every way. German socialism, German philosophy, German science and art forced themselves on the attention, on the admiration, and, let us say the word, on the worship of all peoples. This propaganda had in its service the qualities of the race: organization, stubbornness, profound reflection and work. It has been said a hundred times and it is indisputable: "Ten years yet, and Germany was mistress of the world." God did not allow it. Military power, under the protection of which Greater Germany grew, ceaselessly instigated the greed for universal domination; it formed a predatory nation which wanted to hasten the quarry that it had dreamed of for so long a time. This war, prepared and criminally orchestrated, was thus decided. It is a cataclysm which here we envisage only as a giant step in the march of the world towards the end times and the reign of Antichrist.

We are almost astounded when we consider the ideas and the things which this war pushed so quickly to maturity. The possible realities, which formerly seemed to us distant and as though in a dream, suddenly got closer to the point of being palpable. What did we see in fact? The possibility of a more complete universal domination than that aspired to by the conquerors of all the ages. The unity of the world under the Roman power prepared for the first advent of Christ; the second will be preceded by the reign of the Antichrist which will be frightening in a different way. All peoples will be bent under a power controlling, as much as God will allow it, the forces of nature and the resources of a civilization fruitful in prodigies. The progress made for the last 100 years has accelerated in the last 25 years in breathtaking proportion: railroads with fast trains, highways with driving, airways with aviation; steam, electricity, rays of all kinds; chemical, ballistic and mechanical sciences; surgery and medical science. What do we see and what we shall see in twenty years? But it is the state which seizes all the social forces, penetrates everywhere, and regulates everything. Military service reaches all individuals and subjects them, wherever they may be in the world, by a constraint of the body which can be long-lasting. Monopolies and transports, the family, associations and orphans, sales and purchases, bread and all food, lighting and heating: everything, finally, is in the power of the State in a measure still unsuspected, but which war suddenly brought about. Ancient slavery returned under the name of civil mobilization with terrible prospects for the future; and requisitions of every sort singularly weakened the idea and the rights of individual property.

Until this day, the inhabitants of a nation found refuge abroad. This war has almost demolished borders. Nations are reunited, pervade one another, and consult for concerted action and identical procedures. Abroad the laws and obligations of one's country are no longer escaped: and they speak of sending every foreigner back to his country or of subjecting him to the laws of the country that he lives in.

Military service was the aim here, but other purposes can be pursued. We have now, then, a clear vision of a power locking up the people of the earth under its authority, in their exterior life as well as in the intimacy of the family and of their conscience. And the day when the State will try to transform tickets and necessary papers for traveling, eating, selling and buying, into a sign of apostasy, to put *the mark of the Beast*, then will be realized the prediction of the Apocalypse; and there will only be two alternatives: deny one's baptism or die, to adore Christ or bend in front of satan: *Haec omnia tibi dabo, si cadens adoraveris me.*

There have been wars in every time, and periods of peace are rare, short and not universal. But by giving as precursory signs of His coming wars and rumors of wars: "And you shall hear of wars and rumours of wars" [Mt. 24:6], the Savior suggested to us sufficiently that these wars would have the proportions of a cataclysm; and the one of 1914 is, indeed, a world cataclysm, such as had never been seen. If a time must come where disasters will have had no equals in the history of the world, it is necessary to acknowledge that ours is getting a lot closer to it. Nations are disrupted down to the foundation of their life: "Nations were troubled, and kingdoms were bowed down" [Ps. 45:7]. They are mobilized all at once, thrown outside their normal state, militarized even in their civil life; they are on the brink of numerous abysses: abysses of finance, industry, and depopulation. And it is all the nations, not only the belligerents who entered this world war, but also some others were more or less imprisoned in their precarious neutrality.

What especially has to draw our attention, is that this war is satanic; it is basically a religious war. Doubtless, in unleashing it, Germany wanted to realize its dream of universal dominance, as Prussia, which governs it, had established its own in 1870 in the German states. But, for universal Masonry, this is only a step. There is nothing here to guess or to prophesy, we have only to gather by the handfuls what German writers and the Lodges of several countries have emphatically declared and for a long time; to substitute by victorious Germany Lutheranism for Catholicism; to group the Protestant sects in the hand of Caesar, to harness Catholicism, to replace Latin culture, which comes from Rome, with Germanic culture, and to set its science against the dogmas of the former. Then someone will huff and puff on Protestantism, which is only a shadow, a ghost, and that will be the end of Christianity. It will be the era of the brotherhood of the peoples by this *Society of Nations* that already, even in the midst of war, Masonry proposed with a symbolic flag. This brotherhood of the peoples replacing the one that Christendom formed under the authority of the Roman Pontiff will be based on naturalism, the sin of satan; it will be exalted in front of Christ. It will be the end; but already as it clearly declared itself in the stage which we are passing through, in the current war, that Germany did it on orders from the Lodges! What a cry of satanic pride it is: *Germany over everything*, understood, as the writers, politicians and leaders of this country comment on it! Above not only other nations, but everything without exception; over any spiritual power, any revelation, any law, and any right other than its own. From the sphere of the ideas, this principle, this *leitmotif* of the individual or national life, has gone over into deeds and has been applied who knows how.

What a figure of the antichrist and of his power is the figure of the German Caesar formerly at the head of his empire enslaved to his will, drunk with his strength, bewitched by the superman and where everything becomes colossal and superhuman! Superhuman is this pride which rejects any divine and human law, associates God with its crimes, and joins Him with our friend Luther and the old gods of pagan Germany. Superhuman these unheard of and frightful strategies for combat, these murderous and barbaric inventions, these removals of populations, these gigantic devastations, these tyrannical processes of government. Superhuman, as much as inhuman, are these onslaughts where thousands and thousands of human lives are sacrificed without counting.

Neither the perversity of man, nor the qualities and defects of the race are enough to explain these horrors. It is necessary to recognize in it *the depths of satan* [Apoc. 2:24], the spirit of the one who was a murderer from the beginning; they are scenery and props of apocalyptic grandeur with visions of hell.

Will this war be the last one? It is not likely; but then what will the next one be and to what point will it drive us into the disasters of the end times?

The list of the signs preceding the end of the world and the coming of Christ also includes the conversion of the Jews and the reconstitution of their nation in Palestine. A hundred years ago, this return may have been among the hopes of a part of the Jewish nation, but this prospect remained in the obscure depths of a distant future. The Zionist movement hardly dates back thirty years, and behold, at one leap, as a result of the current war, it passes into the foreground, in the same rank of current events as the conditions of peace. The conquest of Jerusalem by the English army allows us to envisage this return as a fact of contemporary history. No doubt the question is complex; the emigration in Palestine is still only partial, and the constitution of a Jewish state is a work fraught with difficulties. We see, however, the beginning of the events which our forefathers considered more remote, and their consummation can deceive our shortsighted forecasts in view of disruptions such as those of which we are witnesses.

Without adding to these signs, without going into even greater detail, it does not seem as if St. Louis-Marie de Montfort could indicate as being near the end times on the threshold of which he lived, we have reason to think that we have entered it and are notably advancing toward it. How many years or even centuries remain for us to live through? Let us not think of specifying it; because the day of the Lord will surprise us like a thief: "The day of the Lord shall so come, as a thief in the night" [1 Th. 5:2]. It is enough not to reject disdainfully the opinion of those who, in the light of some events, conjecture that the world is hastening to its end and that the return of Christ is being prepared. But what is important for us to conclude from these considerations, is that it is necessary to make our own the extraordinary virtues and works of the apostles announced by Montfort; because if the current time is among the end times, let us be at least up to the demands of the mission that God asks of us.

Chapter II

The Virgin Mary and the End Times

Several times, in the pages that we are studying, St. Louis-Marie de Montfort affirms that according to the divine plan, Mary must be more known, better loved and served. He even says that "God, then, wishes to reveal and discover Mary, the masterpiece of His hands, in these latter times" [*True Devotion*]. The expression is bold, because it announces such an increase of glory for Mary, that in comparison with what has preceded, it will be like the discovery of a work, otherwise unknown, and at least still imperfectly appreciated. According to the Saint, this progress in the knowledge of the Blessed Virgin and in the manifestation of her role is connected with the end times of which it is a sign. This is a view proper to the Saint, the importance of which could not be underestimated. It is the subject of this chapter.

Between St. John the Evangelist and St. Louis-Marie de Montfort there are very interesting resemblances that have been too little studied until now. They are two beloved sons of the Virgin Mary, who lived in an intimate union with Her and who consecrated themselves to Her service in a distinctive way and to an unusual extent. The blessed and so grave hour in which the Apostle received Mary into the intimacy of his house and his life did not inaugurate his relations of filial love and of devoted services to the Mother of Jesus. The beloved disciple of the Master was also the beloved disciple of the Mother; and we could point out in the Gospel several indications of these relations before the scene of Calvary. The fact of having, alone among the apostles, accompanied Mary there, sufficiently shows the bonds which united them. In this point the resemblance between Montfort and St. John is complete. The motto which summarizes the life and apostolate of the Saint: *Totus tuus ego sum, et omnia mea tua sunt*, were repeated in other words *accepit eam discipulus in sua* by the apostle St. John.

Now, behold, the Queen of prophets made a similar gift to these two beloved sons: she gave them prophetic insights into the end times, particularly in what concerns her, that is to say, on the role God assigns her in these final battles and in the triumphant return of Christ. These insights, however, although similar in their object, differ in nuanced ways in one writer and the other.

Commentators explain how the Apostle, in his Gospel, rises in a first flight above creatures up to bosom of the Father in order to contemplate the Word: *In principio erat Verbum.* It is also in these heavenly heights, in these splendors of the divinity that the vision of the Apocalypse is offered to St. John, in which the Blessed Virgin appeared to him. He saw her as the Woman clothed with the sun, with the moon under her feet and crowned with twelve stars. Her battle with the dragon takes place, it is true, here on earth; but it is retraced under grandiose and mysterious figures which keep our eyes between Heaven and earth. Mary fights against satan, but as a Sovereign who dominates the attacks and rages of the dragon, as well as the course of events.

St. Louis-Marie de Montfort is inspired by this vision which retraces the history of the Church Militant; but he considers the realization of it according to the operations of divine Wisdom of which Mary is the throne. He was acquainted with the insights of this Wisdom, which in Its works reaches from one end to the other and knows how to bind the end to the beginning: *attingens a fine usque ad finem.* In the direction of things as well as persons, nothing can hinder its simultaneously sweet and strong power: *fortiter suaviterque disponens omnia.* It is in this special light that he contemplates Mary and her providential role. It is by Her, he said, that the Savior came into this world by becoming Man, and it is she who will also prepare His second coming at the end of time. Then, she will battle the dragon, the ancient Serpent; but this will not be a simple episode of her life, an accidental meeting; this will be the continuation and the completion of her divine mission; because God placed her, from the earthly Paradise on, as the personal adversary of satan whose head she will finally crush. This fullness of perspective, which simultaneously embraces the past and the future, which connects the last ages of the world to the first and shows us in all its extent the plan of divine Wisdom for Mary, is assuredly of an extraordinary originality and magnificence; and this is why among so many other prophetic views those of St. Louis-Marie de Montfort stand out. A quick look at the history of the Church will show us how the glory of Mary and her battle against the infernal serpent has progressed at the same time in the course of the ages.

In Christian antiquity, liturgical poetry, the discourses of Christian orators and their writings celebrate, in the East as in the West, the praises of the Blessed Virgin. It is literature where Marian doctrine is set forth with piety, grace, and magnificence.

It was in part inspired by the battle against the heresies. Indeed, after the violence of the persecutions, the ancient Serpent employed deception: *Serpens erat callidior cunctis animantibus terrae*. He tried to bite the heel of the Woman and sometimes attacked her human maternity, sometimes her virginity, and sometimes her divine maternity.

God, Who reserves to Mary the victory over all the heresies in the whole world, *cunctas haereses sola interemisti in universo mundo*, illuminated His Church, so that it might teach, in all their splendor, these dogmas so glorious for Mary. Thus finished with an increase of her glory the battles which the dragon fomented against the Woman in the first centuries.

The Fathers and Doctors of the Middle Ages braided a beautiful crown for the Mother of God, while her cult was propagated under multiple titles in innumerable shrines.

But then arose the antichristian empire of Mahomet, predicted by Daniel. Never had Christendom run a danger like that. The invasion progressed all over the world, in all that at least was known of it; and with destruction, ruins and sterilization, it imposed the destruction of Christianity. After the holy places and Constantinople, the sultan threatened Rome and the papacy. It was once more the Virgin Mary who stood against satan, and by the virtue of the Rosary shattered the antichristian power at Lepanto. She did more: even within this empire, she wanted to protect the faithful and snatch them from tyranny by establishing two religious Orders for the ransom of captives. As the battles and troubles of Christendom grew, the power and mercy of Mary were therefore revealed more and more. We are anxious to come to the centuries which are more specially the object of our study, to these modern times which count among the last.

Protestantism had made a great split among the nations by setting up as a rule revolt against the Church, which very quickly engendered religious wars. After the furies of the beast, here again are the ruses of the serpent. The battle against religion resumes with Jansenism and philosophism. The first was hypocritical and respectful; the second, mocking and contemptuous; they worked to destroy the faith in the world: there also the Serpent tried to bite the heel of the Woman by reducing her glory, disputing her privileges, and diminishing devotion to her. It is then that Montfort preached vigorously and criticized indefatigably in his discourses and writings: "God wishes that His holy Mother should be *at present* more known, more loved, more honoured, than she has ever been" [*T.D.*]. And he added: "This, no doubt, will take place, if the predestinate enter, with the grace and light of the Holy Ghost, into the interior and perfect practice which I will disclose to them shortly" [*T.D.*]. It was of the perfect consecration to Mary by the holy slavery that St. Louis-Marie de Montfort spoke; because this devotion was, indeed, to contribute powerfully to make the Blessed Virgin better known, to make her loved more ardently, and to procure for her a more perfect devotion. It is not an invention of his piety. The atmosphere of the environment where he passed his youth was quite imbued with it. Saint-Sulpice and the Oratory, Mother Mechtilde of the Blessed Sacrament and her Congregation, Father Eudes, Fr. Boudon and how many others held in honor, in the spirituality of the 17th century, this holy slavery of Mary. It was reserved for Montfort to popularize this devotion, to give it a fullness until then unknown, to show the solid foundations of it, and to develop the admirable consequences of it on a number of points. Two centuries have passed since his apostolate, and he anticipated us so much that we have to learn from him, with the conviction that the generations to come will understand him better still. In speaking to his contemporaries, however, Montfort knew that his teaching was appropriate for the needs and dangers of his time; he understood that this devotion was marvelously adapted to the events and ideas of his epoch. It was for him more than an excellent practice of piety, more than a well-defined way of spirituality, because he considered it to be supported on the foundations of Christianity. It was the antidote against this spirit of independence which we called the modern spirit, but which was only the hissing of the ancient Serpent. So clear-sighted, however, was Montfort with regard to his epoch, so pressing were his calls to the fight against the enemies of God, that it is particularly on the future ages that he fixed his gaze.

"God wishes," he said, "to reveal and discover Mary in these latter times;" and one of the reasons that he gives for this is that the Blessed Virgin "being the way by which Jesus Christ came to us the first time, she will also be the way by which He will come the second time, though not in the same manner" [*T.D.*]. Finally, he explains that "Mary must be terrible to the devil and his crew, as an army ranged in battle, principally in these latter times, because the devil, knowing that he has but little time, and now less than ever, to destroy souls, will redouble his efforts and his combats" [*T.D.*]. Behold already what Montfort declared to his epoch; then he adds these remarkable words: "He will presently raise up new persecution, and will put terrible snares before the faithful servants and true children of Mary, whom it gives him more trouble to surmount than it does to conquer others" [*T.D.*]. It is always the persistence of the same insights and their unity. The battle will, indeed, be against God, but also against the Woman and her offspring; and this battle is near. As for these new persecutions, history shows us that, indeed, they soon arrived. The 18th the century, whose beginning Montfort had seen, ended in what we named the great Revolution; great by the extent of its disruptions and the influence of its ideas. It was satanic in its essence; and far from being a sudden, inexplicable storm, it was a work methodically prepared by freemasonry. Neither the empire of Napoleon, nor the governments which succeeded him accomplished the restoration of Christian society in France or elsewhere. There was a time of relative calm, of reconstructions from which religion benefited; but the revolutionary and antireligious ideas were renounced neither by the leaders, nor by the peoples.

They were injected into nations and fermented in them. Universal masonry continued its work and prepared the assault against the Church by varying its tactics to suit the times and countries. Secret societies colluded to put an end to the temporal power of the Popes, in the hope that this blow dealt to the head would lead to the fall of the Church, or at least would facilitate their triumph. That was when the Virgin Mary rose up to confront satan and the dogma of the Immaculate Conception was proclaimed by the Church. How the word of Montfort came true announcing that God wanted His Mother to be more known and better loved than ever! As a result of this definition, Marian theology radiated in all directions new lights, which allowed other lights to be foreseen in the future. But furthermore, in virtue of her Immaculate Conception, the Virgin appeared as the adversary of satan who comes to engage in battle and to give us a guarantee of victory. *Hodie contritum est ab ea caput serpentis antiquae*, chants the Church; and it is to the Immaculate that, on this feast, the Church applies these words of the Apocalypse: "A great sign appeared in Heaven" [Apoc. 12:1]. A prodigy, a sign, a standard (the Latin word has all these meanings which justify the fact in question) appeared in Heaven.

The Christian people were not mistaken there; in seeing this solemn meeting of two adversaries they understood the seriousness of the battle. And because it was to continue more bitterly in France, as the plan of satan was to make the elder daughter of the Church apostatize and to destroy it, it is to the land of France that the Immaculate came to put her virgin foot. She wanted to bring the whole world there so that it could largely draw from the source of graces and so that in view of the supernatural made tangible by miracles, even the lying evidence and the crime of naturalism would become evident. What is the significance of the Lourdes phenomenon? The future will show it to us. How, indeed, can we be mistaken about the providential coincidence of the Eucharistic congress of Lourdes with the declaration of war in 1914? It is a consequence, the consequence that Wisdom puts in its ways. As the moment when the plan of satan was succeeding, by the conspiracy of the Lodges, the Virgin seemed to say: "Have confidence; I am the Immaculate, I preside over events to direct them and I have the mission of conquering satan." The future, let us not doubt it, will show us how the glory and power of Mary will increase still, because all generations will call her blessed.

But what is important to notice, is that as time marches on, as events unfold, as the battle becomes widespread and intensified, the Marian devotion of St. Louis-Marie de Montfort, already so well adapted to the needs of his time, spreads in a surprising way and proves to be a weapon of choice in the hands of the children of the Virgin. Surprising fact! This devotion, seemingly intended only for devout souls and small chapels, is also revealed as a devotion of battle, a means to fight under Mary's standard with appropriate weapons. So-called modern ideas, hatched by the breath of satan, now yield the fruits of their maturity. Personal interpretation succeeds in freeing itself from all dogma and authority, religious or other; naturalism and secularism go hand in hand with revolutionary socialism: all this is condensed in the formula: "Neither God, nor master."

Now what a direct blow to satanic pride is this filial and total dependence, this holy slavery of Mary which Montfort preaches! The soul which consecrates itself to it lives by a profound faith and becomes established in a very pure supernatural atmosphere, which protects it from naturalism even in the privacy of its mind and heart. Consider also how this homage to the royalty of Mary prepares for the reign of Christ in souls and His coming into the world: *Ut adveniat regnum tuum, adveniat regnum Mariae*. We truly do not exaggerate by saying that if St. Ignatius and St. Teresa were opposed in the designs of Providence to Luther and Protestantism, later, in the battle of the Woman against the serpent, Montfort was chosen by God to fight Jansenism and the spirit of independence. In his time, this spirit was already blowing as a gale; soon it was going to revolutionize the world.

It would be advisable also to recall for the glory of Blessed Virgin the events which, in the last twenty five years especially, have made her better known and more honored: the Marian congresses are already a tradition; the solemnities of the Rosary, which Leo XIII established "so that in our time of great trials and prolonged storms the Virgin, so often victorious over earthly enemies, might also make us triumph over those of the hell." But this list would take us too far. Let us note that the increase of the glory of Mary and the manifestation of her power over the enemies of God go hand in hand in history, just as Montfort saw and announced it. And how right Fr. Faber was to assert that his writings would have a greater influence in the Church in ages still to come!

What will happen in this century which begins in the middle of these great cataclysms and in an assault of hell up till now unequaled? The assertions of the Saint are clear: "Mary must shine forth more than ever in mercy, in might, and in grace, in these latter times: in mercy, to bring back and lovingly receive the poor strayed sinners who shall be converted and shall return to the Catholic Church; in might, against the enemies of God, idolaters, schismatics, Mahometans, Jews, and souls hardened in impiety, who shall rise in terrible revolt against God to seduce all those who shall be contrary to them, and to make them fall by promises and threats; and, finally, she must shine forth in grace, in order to animate and sustain the valiant soldiers and faithful servants of Jesus Christ, who shall do battle for His interests" [*T.D.*].

The Virgin is already a prelude to these miracles at the end of time by some deeds whose signification escapes those who do not follow attentively the ways of God. We are, moreover, far from knowing most of these deeds. No doubt, as Montfort hints in the lines which precede, there will be among the Jews the descendants of those who were deicides; and they will continue the battle against Christ with all the power of the Judeo-masonic coalition which leads nations. But there will be also – and Montfort recalls it several times – the conversion of Israel, of the sons of Abraham according to the spirit, after the entry of the nations into the bosom of the Church. This miracle of mercy, so often predicted in the Scriptures, anticipated by Mary herself in her *Magnificat*, will not be made without Her. The conversion of Alphonse Ratisbonne, suddenly enlightened by the Blessed Virgin, is more than a private event, if we compare the circumstances where it took place with the ideas of St. Louis-Marie de Montfort. It is the antiphon of a hymn more beautiful than those of the return from captivity, the forerunner of a great movement and the affirmation of Mary's sovereign role in the events of the last ages.

What else? Look at the battle of the Woman and the Serpent as it follows its course and keeps developing in a thousand different incidents. Mary's role in it is affirmed incessantly. Is there not any relation between the predilection of the Blessed Virgin for France, between her recent visits to La Salette, Lourdes, Pontmain and the persecutions, the plots, the efforts of the Masonry against this kingdom of Mary?

Let us also want to pay attention to the sacrilegious parody of the flag of the Sacred Heart invented by the Lodges, which dream of imposing it on the society of Nations. Satan did not forget the Mother whose Son he blasphemes. On the other side is painted Mary's Heart, as the symbol of the feminine principle in nature, explained in a spiritualist and atheistic spirit. It is, with an infernal guile and in a deep hatred which nothing escapes, the opposite of both devotions which ascend in concert to the firmament of souls: the devotion to the Sacred Heart of Jesus and that of the Immaculate Heart of Mary.

Such is the characteristic originality of de Montfort's insights about the end times: they refer everything to Mary as to their main purpose. We shall see it more and more clearly by meditating on what he says about the apostles whom the Virgin is to form for this time so troubled for the Church militant. The portrait which Montfort drew of it and the description of their apostolate fills some pages that we would look for in vain elsewhere. In his *Fiery Prayer*, as well as in his *Treatise on the True Devotion*, these pages offer to the reader some insights as new as they are admirable that we shall not meditate on without profit for our souls.

Chapter III

The Divine Enmities

The reader will indeed want to read again in full the pages where Montfort so strongly sketched the portrait of these apostles whom in the last ages of the Church Mary is to raise up and lead into combat. This portrait deserves that we examine its resemblance trait for trait with the One who is their Queen and Mother. It is like illustrating the text of a written account with photos. Will it not facilitate our study to continue to concretize it at times in the two already familiar figures of St. John and St. Louis-Marie de Montfort? What we know about the similarity of their insights into the end times will become still more accentuated in what we will explain.

In the picture of the end times that Montfort has made for us, what is especially striking, due to its powerful enhancement, is the antagonism of the Virgin and satan established by God Himself at the time of the original fall. The Saint comments on, but with an almost hasty accumulation of forceful thoughts, the famous text of Genesis, which contains, along with curses, the divine promises. It follows that, in its turn, the text of Montfort calls for some explanations.

"I will put enmities between thee and the woman...*Inimicitias ponam inter te et mulierem*" [Gn. 3:15]. This is, remarks the Saint, the only enmity God has *made* and *formed*. Let us scrutinize these two words of profound meaning. God did not only permit this enmity; He made it. It is His work; and just as at the beginning of creation He separated light from darkness – *divisit lucem a tenebris*, – thus He did between Mary and the serpent, as well as between their offspring.

This work, like all the works of God, reflects His perfections. He gave it a *form* such as He wanted in His wisdom: this enmity would be by nature total, indomitable and eternal.

It is total, because "God has not only set an enmity but enmities, antipathies, and secret hatreds" [*T.D.*]. This emphatic plural: *inimicitias* is employed in sacred Scripture, as elsewhere, to indicate a thing carried to its highest degree, to its maximum intensity. An enmity can weaken or disappear, it can contain exceptions: all of which would be improbable, if it is a matter of a bundle of enmities more difficult to break, as it is a triple link: "A threefold cord is not easily broken" [Eccle. 4:12]. This bundle is composed of successive manifestations of enmity in time or multiplied by their diverse applications: antagonism in ideas, intentions and feelings; antagonism in love or hatred, in purpose as well as in means, in joys and sadness; antagonism, finally, in the life of individuals as well as in that of societies.

Inimicitias ponam. This verb: *put, found, establish*, "*ponam*", expresses the solidity of the divine work, in nature as in grace. So, then, having been placed by God, this enmity is so firm that it is unyielding or absolute. It is the opposition of Being and nothingness, of truth and error, of good and evil, of love and hatred, in which are reflected the absolute of the divine Being, His purity, and His transcendence.

And, consequently, this enmity is eternal, like the love which is opposed to it, because God is eternal. This enmity "shall endure and develop even to the end" [*T.D.*].

Ah! If God wants His holy Mother to be better known and glorified, did not Montfort make her shine with a greater light by showing how this spotless mirror – *speculum sine macula* – in her opposition to satan, reflects very purely the divine perfections? Undoubtedly, we will never celebrate enough the goodness of Mary, her mercy, and her maternal love; but let us not forget the hatred which is inseparable from them and follows them. God put it in Her from the beginning, and His infinite holiness is reflected there indulgently.

But the Woman and the Serpent have each their offspring; and between them God wants an unalterable antagonism to be perpetuated: *Inimicitias ponam inter te et mulierem, et semen tuum et semen illius.* This enmity essentially characterizes them, to the point that the measure in which it deteriorates and disappears, men depart from one or the other lineage and no longer live in its spirit. What a great lesson and how fruitful for the Christian life still fighting here on earth! It is, in reality, the purity of faith and holiness of life which are in question.

What is this offspring of the Serpent? They are, says St. Louis-Marie de Montfort, "the children of Belial, the slaves of satan, the friends of the world (for it is the same thing)" [*T.D.*]. Let us be careful not to see in this accumulation of qualifiers a rhetorical device; it is a complete list of the diverse categories which compose the offspring of the serpent. In the first place, they are the children of Belial, of the one who, in his pride, as his name signifies, submits himself to no law. Therefore, the children of Belial are rebels against the Church, revolutionaries of the natural order established by God. Then come the slaves of satan, the innumerable crowd of sinners seduced and enslaved: "Whosoever committeth sin, is the servant of sin" [Jn. 8:34]. Finally, the friends of the world, of this world entirely rooted in evil – "The whole world is seated in wickedness" [1 Jn. 5:19]; of this world which does not acknowledge God: "And the world knew Him not" [Jn. 1:10]; of this world in which there is only "the concupiscence of the flesh, and the concupiscence of the eyes, and the pride of life." *Quoniam omne quod est in mundo concupiscentia carnis est, et concupiscentia oculorum et superbia vitae* [1 Jn. 2:16]. Is there a need to recall the traits which characterize the children of the Virgin, the offspring of the Woman? They are the complete opposite of those whom we have just examined. Many a time the Saint speaks about the humility, obedience, and poverty which distinguish the children of the Virgin and they will shine with a vivid brightness among the apostles that she has to form.

But between the two offspring, just as between the Woman and the Serpent, the enmity placed by God must persist entirely, absolutely, implacably, and consequently, eternally. No association is possible between light and darkness, no accord between Christ and Belial [cf. 2 Cor. 6:15]. If the race of the Serpent does not cease to persecute that of the Woman, this one not only has to avoid, but to hate evil and guard with jealous care the intransigence of the faith against error. How can we forget that if satan is the cruel animal, the prowling lion seeking whom he may devour, he is also the serpent without equal in cunning – *callidior cunctis animantibus terrae.*

Now this absolute separation of the two lineages, which is in the logic of the divine enmities, is insupportable for him. It is for him as a stigma revealing his state, a dishonor and an obstacle to his enterprises. It asserts God with His infinite perfections and His over against his condition as a fallen creature; it is the prolonged echo of that *who is like to God,* which precipitated his fall into the abyss; it proclaims that God is good, and that he is an evil and condemned angel. If God permits him to battle still on earth at the head of those who are of his race and moved by his spirit, at least by keeping separate the two lines, as formerly Israel and the pagan nations were, God protects in His beloved sons the integrity of the faith and the knowledge of good; He puts His people outside the reach of satan.

If only this enmity was not unchanging and as a consequence eternal! If it could be modified, diminished, and finally disappear! But no! The immutability of the divine Being, Who is truth, goodness, and holiness, renders unchanging also the condition of the fallen angel. He remains eternally damned in the face of heavenly beatitude, darkness in face of light, error and falsehood against the truth, the evil spirit opposed to good, death attacking life, the accursed being who is rejected forever from the face of the Lord. Always then, between him and God, between him and this Woman that God opposes to him and whom he abhors, "that he fears," says Montfort, "not only more than all angels and men, but in some sense more than God Himself," between his offspring and hers, this enmity will persist along with this battle in which he will finally be conquered. This fixedness irritates his hatred and causes his torment. So as in every time he fought her, mixing craftiness with boldness, according to his usual manner! Never were this satanic work and its results so universal and deep as in our time. How can we not see in them a sign of these times which will precede the return of Christ, and in which, under the spell of the seductions of satan, the faith will be lost and charity will grow cold because of the multitude of sins?

Jesus Christ said that He came to bring to earth not peace, but the sword [cf. Mt. 10:34], by alluding to these battles between the two offspring. He is, however, the Prince of peace, *Princeps pacis*, says Isaiah; He gives peace to His own, a true and total peace which will be consummated in eternal happiness. But, just as he wants to substitute himself for God, the eternal Light which rises from the East, and because he tries hard to steal this title and its symbols, fallen Lucifer also makes himself Prince of peace with regard to the divine enmities. Here is the source of this pacifism which he would like to establish especially and, first of all, in religious matters, in ideas as in deeds, for individuals and for nations; and the mirage is all the more attractive as the upheavals are deeper and the battles more dreadful. The Middle Ages, when there was no lack of wars and misfortunes, prayed that the Lord might put an end to it. With the Church, it gave in its liturgical prayer a large part to peace; but it never dreamed about this peace outside of God. After the religious wars and the horrors of the Revolution, which were manifestations of the violent hatred against God, the Serpent used guile and falsehood to deceive men, to weaken and debilitate the enmity on which God establishes religion and which is the armature of the Christian faith. It is a phenomenon characteristic of our modern times.

Religious peace? Christianity effects it by the union of souls in the same faith and divine charity, and by their meeting in the same fold under the leadership of the divine Shepherd. Satan proposes it by the abolition of any enmity, any mutually exclusive antagonism between error and truth, between revelation and independent reason, called free thinking. No more fights, no more barriers, unbridgeable because of the fixedness of dogmas and the inflexibility of the divine or ecclesiastical laws. It is religious tolerance in minds as in the acts of life. Subtle poison and not without its charms, a perfect and progressive anesthetic, a sleeping sickness which invades the soul whose vitality and strengths it saps. A famous apostate summarized this peace in two words: skepticism and sweetness. They are, he said, two exquisite virtues. We saw this tolerance unfurl in learned theses of intellectuals, or being coined for the people into striking aphorisms: "All religions are good; all have to fraternize: the Church no longer has to demand more than the common law; the truth is entitled to no privilege. And then what is the truth? *Quid est veritas?*"

The 19th century abundantly drank this magic beverage whose most vaunted distiller was Renan. Spiritual anemia ensued. Do we not indeed see religious opinions and feeling too often replacing the vigor of faith and the hatred of evil?

But the current war shook this lethargy and exposed the error which we did not want to recognize. For any right, sound, and truly Christian mind, it is the fatal outcome of godless doctrines, of a civilization without God, of a social state in which religious neutrality is henceforth considered legitimate; it is the punishment for the blasphemy, crimes, and persecutions against the Church, which people have ended up siding with. The thunderclap shook everything, and the lesson was so clear that under the first impression the religious movement was considerable. There was an awakening of faith and a lessening of evil. Was God going to triumph? With his intelligence and guile, satan understood that, violence no longer being opportune, it was necessary to put to sleep and anesthetize at all costs the patient who was waking up; and the watchword of Masonry was the appeal to the holy alliance. Hypocritical formula, like those that it specializes in, which could be understood according to order, but was interpreted and applied in quite a different spirit. It was launched by a minister who had uttered from the height of the speaker's platform this proud challenge: "With a broad gesture we put out the lights of Heaven which will no longer be rekindled." And the One Who dwells in Heaven and laughs at the impious twisted, by a divine irony, his blasphemy by obliging him to veil the lights of the earth. Even Paris saw itself putting out the enchanting sights of its lights, and for a long time remained plunged in darkness which too often were furrowed by other murderous lights.

What is, then, this holy alliance? It is, in sum, satanic pacifism in ideas and acts, the suppression of any necessary antagonism, fraternization in the abdication of the rights of truth, God, and His Church. To do this, the homeland is alleged to be over everything. Is it not itself the only true religion which has to unite all wills? For heaven's sake, let sin no longer be spoken of, especially national sin, nor the punishment which follows it, so as not to upset the sinner and the impious. Even prayer ordered by the ecclesiastical authority was to this end censored and truncated. Holy alliance! As if something could be holy without God, and much less against Him! Unless we give to this word the execrable and cursed meaning, as in the *auri sacra fames* of the Latin poet. So matured in the midst of war, like so many other things, the religious tolerance of the previous century.

But to bring together, to weaken, and to distort is only one step. Satan cannot content himself with it; he wants to destroy this enmity, to eliminate this antagonism which keeps him away and sets the divine strengths against him. Then with this boldness which, after his insidious questions, abruptly made him deny the divine threat which Eve objected to him: *Nequaquam moriemini*, he no longer contents himself with compromises and tolerance; he completely urges his lie against God. If there is in time an opposition, an antagonism, this does not keep to the essence of things, or to the divine Being, and will not last eternally. A day will come where both principles, good and evil, will become reconciled; where hell will finally end and return its inhabitants to the celestial dwelling; where error and truth will merge; where good and evil will meet in complete peace. Thus, the judgment after death decides nothing, and does not settle the fate of men irrevocably. After the wanderings of metempsychosis or without them, everything will end by being absorbed in God: just men and sinners, good or evil works. Nothing more is unchanging; everything evolves: the earth and Heaven, religion and God Himself. Then, why should there be enmities and battles? How can we establish them on what does not last and changes perpetually?

Manichaeism had favored these infernal seductions, which nowadays reappear dressed in new formulas and propagated by new or renewed stratagems. The theories of evolution or of *perpetual becoming* gained widespread acceptance. Then occultism, spiritualism, and modern metempsychosis or reincarnation recruit followers. There, if there is still talk of a kind of necessary purification, *in the shadowy corners*, where for a time souls are relegated, you will never hear about hell, eternal damnation, and good and fallen angels. These dogmas assert explicitly or by way of logical inference the complete religion and reveal satan such as he is. Did not we see right minds turning to God and believing in Him, because at first they had believed in the devil? Inevitable and salutary logic of the antagonisms placed by God and which the Serpent tries hard to fight at all costs. He does it even at the cost of reason, the fundamental notions of which he destroys to this end and denies its most evident operations. This is the infernal work of German philosophy, more formidable by its inexplicable seduction than by the violence of military power. This smoke which rose from the well of the abyss, more deadly and more widespread over the world than the poison gases inaugurated by Germany, corroded the roots of reason and faith. They are indeed anti-

Christian and anti-intellectual principles; this subjectivism and this egocentrism, above all, this identity of the I and the not-I and generally of all opposites; this agnosticism about cause and effect relationships; these anesthetic formulas: *areligious*, *amoral*, instead of atheistic and immoral. No clashes, no antagonism. But they are, however, the shameless lies of the one who is the prince of them, because in this respect *to omit* is just as criminal as *to commit*, the two are equivalent. From the breath of satan, these toxic fumes more or less penetrated even among the faithful. From where comes this repugnance to hear about hell and eternal punishments? Do not we remember famous discussions about St. Athanasius's Creed and its final penalties? We cannot doubt the spirit which inspired them.

There is more still; because it is not only over individuals, but also over nations that satan wants to reign against Christ to Whom God gave them as an inheritance. And always and everywhere, if he rises against the divine laws, against the order established by God, it is by advocating peace; but we can rightly apply here the saying of the Latin historian: wherever he causes devastation and death to reign, satan proclaims that there is peace. Peace of conscience, when there is no longer a conscience; peace in the reason, when it no longer reasons; peace in the mind, when there is no longer truth nor light; peace in the family, when there is no longer a family because of divorce and voluntary sterility; peace in nations, when patriotism will have disappeared from it and when all will be dissolved and subjected to his power. Here is the purpose of this League of Nations which is presently working to organize international Freemasonry. Thus do events march towards this reign of the antichrist, which will mark the end of time.

May the immaculate Virgin deign to preserve in the souls of her priests and apostles the understanding and feeling of these implacable enmities. May this most pure and faithful Virgin safeguard in them the integrity of an energetic and unalloyed hatred, which alone can guarantee the purity of their faith and the fidelity of their love for Christ. He who allows them to weaken begins to deny his baptism and his Christian life; because just as God put these enmities at the beginning of the world, He also requires them as a condition of baptismal regeneration, and we only become a child of God by hating satan: *Abrenuntio satanae? Abrenuntio.*

In order to perfect this Christian life, in order to give Mary the most abandoned souls, what, then, does St. Louis-Marie de Montfort ask? Nothing other than to renew and perfect this enmity. "I have hated them with a perfect hatred, and they are become enemies to me" [Ps. 138:22]. In the formula of his consecration to Jesus by the hands of Mary, he opposes "to the cruel slavery of the devil" the holy slavery of Mary and the renewal of baptismal promises. It is to get a foothold irrevocably on the other bank, with all bridges being cut; it is decidedly to line up on the side of God, confronting the enemy. And what will be the fruit of this total donation? The Saint enumerates, in the first place, a greater participation in the faith of Mary: "a faith animated by charity…, a faith immovable as a rock…, a faith to resist the devil and all the enemies of salvation" [*T.D.*].

This faith which animated Montfort is exalted in sublime accents in his *Fiery Prayer*. It is his own portrait that he draws in that of the apostles of the end times, fearless fighters whom he encourages by his rhetoric until the final victory. Nowhere do we see in his writings or in his life a trace of compromise, accommodations, or weakening in his enmities against the world and satan. How could there be any, since, at the end of the battle, Mary will crush the head of the serpent? "She shall crush thy head" [Gen 3:15]: it the word of God Himself against which hell will not prevail.

Thus will be the apostles raised by Mary: "…clouds thundering and flying through the air…They shall thunder against sin; they shall storm against the world; they shall strike the devil and his crew; and they shall strike further and further, for life or for death, with their two-edged sword of the Word of

God, all those to whom they shall be sent on the part of the Most High" [*T.D.*].

This is certainly not the portrait of the pontiffs of the false peace of whom satan is the prince. On the other hand, we recognize in it St. Louis-Marie de Montfort of whom these lines summarize the apostolate so characterized.

Also, indeed, of the offspring of the Woman and imbued with her spirit was this beloved disciple, who was St. John. Right from the beginning of his Gospel, he clearly separates those who are born of flesh and blood from those who are children of God. No connection between the two races is suggested by him. His epistles are full of anathemas against the world and of vehement condemnations against heresies and heresiarchs. When finally in his Apocalypse, in which there would be so much to bring out, he makes heard the mutual sighs of Bridegroom and Spouse who call each other, when he speaks about this coming of Jesus which will be the triumph and the reward of the just, it is after having excluded from Heaven cynics, poisoners, the "unchaste, and murderers, and servers of idols, and every one that loveth and maketh a lie" [Apoc. 22:15]. Thus will the enmity placed by God at the beginning be consummated by an eternal and complete separation. Just like Christ, Who is the cause of it, this enmity too is the alpha and the omega of sacred Scripture. Proclaimed from the first pages in order to punish original sin and cure it, it asserts itself at the end as the conclusion of the redemptive work and the triumph of the Church militant. And it is St. John, the Evangelist of love, the apostle *par excellence* of divine charity, who announces this final judgment of the consummated enmity, definitive separation and eternal damnation. "Without are dogs, and sorcerers, and unchaste, and murderers, and servers of idols, and every one that loveth and maketh a lie" [Apoc 22:15].

Chapter IV

"As your children and your slaves" [St. Louis-Marie de Montfort]

It is in this capacity that Montfort asks us to consecrate ourselves if we wish to practice the perfect devotion that he teaches. Will he ask less of these great servants of the Blessed Virgin, these apostles of the end times? Assuredly not; because he insistently repeats that they "will consecrate themselves entirely to her service, as subjects and slaves of love…they will love her tenderly like well-beloved children" [*T.D.*]. Here is what will especially characterize them; because their other distinctive traits will only be the accompaniment or the blossoming of that one. Is it not necessary for them to be more animated by the spirit of Mary and more possessed by Her, these elect children who, in the battle, will also be her best instruments? Therefore, see how they are in special connection with the Blessed Virgin, those who, in all ages and periods of intense crisis, fought for God or who were precursors by preparing the ways of Christ. It is Elias in his battles against Achab and idolatry. His name is inseparable from Carmel where he saw the light cloud, a type of the Virgin. There was the cradle of the public cult of Mary in the nascent Church. At the end of time, he has to return to fight again and dispose men for the Second Coming of the Lord. Then, undoubtedly, his symbolic vision of the cloud will be explained and will blossom in wonderful realities. It will appear that the spirit and the strength of Elias (*in spiritu et virtute Eliae*) come to him from the Virgin victorious over the dragon.

Here is John the Baptist, the precursor of Christ. According to the word of the angel, he was to go before Him *in the spirit and power of Elias* [Lk. 1:17], to prepare a perfect people for the Lord. But how can we forget that it is by Mary's visit that John, still in his mother's womb, was filled with the Holy Spirit, Who flowed back to Elizabeth from him? "It is by Mary," says St. Louis-Marie de Montfort, "that (in this circumstance) Jesus worked His first and greater miracle of grace; just as at the wedding of Cana He worked His first miracle of nature." Then, like Elias, completely filled with the spirit of Mary, John proved in his childhood to be austere, strong, separated from the world and living in the desert. Finally, as to Elias, Mary communicated to him her power: *in spiritu et virtute*. The parallelism between his apostolate and that of the prophet of the Old Law is remarkable. Far from making a pact with evil, they hate it and pursue it even unto the peril of their life, the one against Achab, the other against Herod. Their apostolates are accomplished *virtute multa*, because miracles abound in them. Elias divides the waters of the Jordan; John baptizes the crowds in it; and soon Jesus will descend in the sacred river where, after His baptism, God will manifest Him to the crowds which listen to the Precursor.

The apostles of the end times will also come *in the spirit and power of Mary*; of Mary, who will choose and form them by renewing for them what she did in Elias and St. John the Baptist. There is no question here of an ordinary or even a fervent devotion; because these apostles who are destined for incredible combats, in a time in which everything will march to its consummation, good as well as evil, must be possessed and moved by the spirit of Mary, invested with her power to a degree still unknown. Montfort asserts it in clear terms, which are not unsurprising at first sight. Having said that the greatest saints, the souls most rich in graces and virtues, will be the ones most devoted to the Blessed Virgin, he adds: "I have said that this would come to pass particularly at the end of the world, and indeed presently, because the Most High with His holy Mother has to form for Himself great Saints, who shall surpass most of the other Saints in sanctity, as much as the cedars of Lebanon outgrow the little shrubs" [*T.D.*].

Not satisfied with this overview, Montfort specifies the details; he not only sketches a silhouette, he elaborates the portrait, by commenting on these two words: *in spiritu et veritate*. "These souls shall be singularly devoted to our Blessed Lady, illuminated by her light, nourished by her milk, led by her spirit, supported by her arm, and sheltered under her protection..." [*T.D.*]. "They (these true children and servants of Mary) will be little and poor in the world's esteem...but rich in the grace of God, which Mary shall distribute to them abundantly, great and exalted before God in sanctity" [*T.D.*]. They will consecrate themselves entirely to this Sovereign, as her children and slaves of love [cf. *T.D.*]. "They will deliver themselves to Mary, body and soul, without reserve, that they may thus be all for Jesus Christ" [*T.D.*]. This is the sort of spirit that will possess these great servants.

Here now is the power of their apostolate: *Et virtute.* The power of Mary over all demons will shine forth particularly in the end times, when satan will lie in wait for her heel, that is to say, for these humble slaves and poor children that she will arouse to wage war against him..."In union with Mary, they shall crush the head of the devil, and cause Jesus Christ to triumph...They will be sharp arrows in the hand of the powerful Mary to pierce her enemies...They shall be clouds thundering and flying through the air at the least breath of the Holy Ghost...They shall be the true apostles of the latter times, to whom the Lord of Hosts shall give the word and the might to work marvels, and to carry off the glory of the spoils of His enemies" [*T.D.*].

Such will be these apostles that the Saint saw in the future advancing with the crucifix in their right hand and the rosary in their left. What principally distinguishes them is their consecration to Mary. He undoubtedly knew that these future apostles would not appear as isolated and transient meteors. They belong to a lineage, to the offspring of the Woman that he saw continuing in history from the beginning. Closer to him, the figure of St. Dominic was familiar to him, as well as that of saint Vincent Ferrer; and it is to assert his connection and his communion of thought with them that he wanted to be affiliated with the Dominican family through the Third Order. What he saw in these great servants of Mary, his predecessors, he shows in those who will succeed him, but with a kind of intensification and perfection, with a revival in compliance with the end times when everything will be taken to the extreme and will be consummated.

The satisfaction of the watchman, which persistently scrutinizes the still too foggy horizon and sees it clearing up, is similar to the one we experience in discovering little by little the beauties of the Marian devotion which Montfort preaches. Let us not diminish its impact. Doubtless the main purpose of his small *Treatise* is to explain its nature, to put aside the errors and abuses which can disfigure it, to popularize the practice of it in every degree for the sanctification of souls; and in this order of ideas he teaches a way of asceticism and even mysticism about which, in spite of everything we have already written, there remains much to say. From the first pages, however, it is in the vast perspectives of the divine plan for the world, it is in relation to the two comings of Christ and the destiny of holy Church that he speaks to us of Mary and her great servants. Of these he forgets nothing, neither their interior life, nor their apostolate. Their perfect consecration to Mary is the crucible where their soul will be purified with a view to their combats. To these apostles, successors of those who, at Pentecost, had grouped around Mary, Montfort does not hesitate to recognize in them the characteristic traits of the mysterious animals of Ezechiel: "They will be men by their great charity; they will be courageous like lions; they will have the strength of an ox and the agility of the eagle."

There are two great things, moreover, closely connected, which dominate the life of the Church militant, namely, the development of dogma and piety, in its interior life; and, in its exterior life, its fights against the offspring of the Serpent. These two things command our attention for an understanding of the great world crises which, with regard to ideas as well as actions, are the turning points of history. Now, it is among these major things, among these guiding causes, that the Marian devotion of St. Louis-Marie of Montfort takes its place. This is what groups and forms the sons of the Virgin in a battalion of the elect, in "*a picked handful of the predestined*"; by this devotion Mary will be better known and more perfectly served; the prodigious graces reserved for the end times will be poured on the world in a torrent, and, finally, the triumphant return of the Lord will be prepared. Therefore, this profound thinker, Fr. Faber, exaggerated nothing when he wrote: "I cannot think of a higher work or a broader vocation for any one than the simple spreading of this peculiar devotion" [Preface of the English edition].

The sublimity of this doctrine constitutes the glory of the master who teaches it, and the greatness of the work that it produces is on a par with that of the worker. Only the keen eyesight and the high flight of the eagle which St. John had, allowed him to soar higher than these views which are so clear, so vast and so perfect. In that, these two privileged sons of Mary are likened, who were similar also in their devotion and their dedication to this holy Mother.

These considerations are enough to classify as unrivalled St. Louis-Marie de Montfort, who, in other respects, could be compared to holy personages and great missionaries. His glory will grow in proportion as Mary's glory will grow; and, in the course of events, his insights and teaching will acquire a striking timeliness.

During the troubled days in which we live, those people who are in contact with what can be called the world of souls, where we see not undersides, but the tops of events, notice with joy and admiration that numerous are the chosen souls who thirst for justice, dedicated to love and sacrifice for the reign of Jesus and His Church. They are hidden souls, unknown by the world and unknown to themselves. They are the spiritual forces who will overcome material power; they are among these humble, among these little ones who will topple the great and the powerful of this world. Who raises up these souls? The Most Blessed Virgin, as their deeds bear witness. They are abandoned to her by a consecration equivalent to that of the holy slavery, when it is not formulated in the same terms proposed by Montfort. It is, then, Mary who, throughout the world, raises her chosen army and leads them in the battle against satan.

Then how can we not notice that, concerned about the interests of the Church, they are generally concerned about the priesthood; they pray, they devote themselves, they sacrifice themselves to make reparation and to obtain the graces which will cause the apostles to be equal to the mission which God intends for them. Nothing is more consistent with sound teaching, because it is by the priestly ministry that God confers grace and teaches men. Montfort has in mind these auxiliaries of the priesthood who, in multiple ways, contribute to it the help of their interior life and their holy works, and asks for them. "...and makes me hope for a great success...for a great squadron of brave and valiant soldiers of Jesus and Mary, of both sexes, to combat the world, the devil, and corrupted nature in those more than ever perilous times which are about to come" [*T.D.*].

Finally, it is a great and consoling movement which draws priests around Mary and makes them welcome with eagerness the ideas of St. Louis-Marie de Montfort. They consecrate themselves to the Blessed Virgin and want to dwell on this rich and fertile mountain. They are molded in Mary in order to become the apostles who will lead the fight and set themselves up "as a pillar of fire and a wall of brass" [Jer. 1:18] against the enemies of the Lord. It is what we are going to study in the following chapter.

Chapter V

Priests of Mary

Beloved sons of the Virgin Mary and consecrated to her service, that is undoubtedly what St. John and St. Louis-Marie de Montfort were. But when the hour sounded when the Apostle took into his care the Mother of Jesus – *et ex illa hora accepit eam discipulus in sua,* – he was a priest since the day before. The divine Master had conferred on him in the Cenacle the power of consecrating with the order to renew the Eucharistic sacrifice in memory of Him. In his life and among the goods which St. John indicated by these words: *in sua,* there was, therefore, and above all, his priesthood, of which he made an homage to Mary and which he dedicated to her service. In a word, he became the priest of Mary. It is a pious and traditional belief, respectable for its plausibility, that living with the Mother of God, St. John consecrated his ministry to her by celebrating Mass for Her and by giving her holy Communion. In this way, he returned to her Jesus Whose place he took. Happier than the Levites of the old Law, he guarded the holy Ark of the new Covenant; he surrounded it with faith and love, and enclosed God Himself within it. It was more than the rod of Aaron and the tables of the Law. Then, whereas the other apostles dashed across the world to preach the Gospel, his part was to stay near Mary. If he sometimes changed residence, if he went from Ephesus to Jerusalem, it was probably in the company of the Blessed Virgin. How can we not recall the delightful commentary of St. Louis-Marie de Montfort about Jacob and Rebecca? Is not this son, loving his mother and loved by her, who preferred to remain near her, obeyed her in everything and sought only to please her, a figure of St. John once he became the priest of Mary?

In this connection, the so animated life of St. Louis-Marie de Montfort contrasts with that of St. John. But if we look at it closely, we shall notice that this life of apostolic courses is completely in the service of Mary. Like the angels, who in their missions do not lose the beatific vision, Montfort is never diverted from Mary. Sermons and writings, successes or trials, everything came to him from the Virgin or referred to Her. He was her priest and apostle, to the point that it is difficult to find anyone who surpasses him or can even equal him. In that he continued to be what he was from the beginning of his priestly career; because his vocation, according to the testimony of his friend, M. Blain, was a grace of Mary. As a seminarian, he had the care of the altar of the Blessed Virgin at Saint-Sulpice, where he later celebrated his first Mass to pay tribute for his priesthood to this divine Mother. And when he would write his hymns on the Eucharist, Mary would be absent neither from his contemplation, nor from his love.

You priests of the generations who now succeed one another, apostles of the end times which Montfort announces and exhorts, be also priests of Mary in order to carry out your mission. Offer her the homage of your priesthood and dedicate your holy ministry to her.

This will be, in the first place, justice; because if all graces come to us by Mary, how would this excellent grace of the priesthood escape her hands? Jesus, Priest and Victim, is always the Son of the Virgin, and this privileged participation in the mystery of Christ which she obtained for you demands a return.

But this will also be for your unworthiness and weakness a priceless help and a sure safeguard. For a long time priestly piety has invoked Mary under the title *Queen of the clergy*. That of *Virgin priest* is the object of serious studies which, by putting aside doctrinal errors and thoughtless devotion, allows priests to seek in Mary a model and way to unite with Jesus the High Priest.

A worthy custom in all respects invites priests, on the feast of the Presentation of Mary, to renew their clerical promises; but it seems that the mystery of the Presentation of Jesus in the Temple and the Purification of Mary are suited better still for a priestly feast. There, indeed, by Mary's hands, Jesus publicly inaugurates His priesthood by offering Himself to His Father. This aspect of the aforementioned mystery is explained by Malachi, whose remarkable prophecy supplied the Epistle of this feast: "And presently the Lord, whom you seek, and the angel of the testament, whom you desire, shall come to his temple" [Mal. 3:1]. But by what right does He enter it and what does He come to do there? He comes to the temple with the title priest and victim to offer Himself, as the true Lamb. He undoubtedly had offered Himself from the first moment of His Incarnation; but this interior and secret oblation which the Scriptures reveal to us was a prelude to this other public offering, which would be like the morning sacrifice in relation to the evening sacrifice consummated on Calvary. Therefore, embracing with a divinely illuminated glance the whole mystery of Christ, His human life as well as His mystical life in the Church, the prophet Malachi announces at the same time the sacrifice of Jesus, divine High Priest, and the Christian priesthood which He will institute in conditions of holiness superior to those of the old Law. That is why, after having spoken about the sanctified people that could be compared to refined silver, the prophet shows the special love and the jealous care with which God, as the artisan seated near the crucible which he watches over, will purify the sons of Levi, who, however, were only the figure of the Christian priesthood. He will cast them drop by drop, no longer only as silver, but as gold, *et colabit eos quasi aurum et quasi argentum*, so that their sacrifices please the Lord as those of past centuries. And echoing the ancient prophecy in order to show the fulfillment of it, the Church recites in the Canon of the Mass the prayer: *Supra quae propitio ac sereno vultu respicere digneris*. In front of the consecrated Host, she combines with the sacrifice of the new Law the ancient sacrifices of Abel, Abraham and Melchisedech, which pleased the Lord. May He deign to approve this Eucharistic oblation, because it too, and more excellently still, is a holy sacrifice and a spotless host!

Let us also scrutinize the depths of the mystery. It is through the hands of Mary that Jesus, the eternal Priest and divine Lamb, comes to offer Himself to God; and it is because in the Temple, as on Calvary, Mary is associated with the priestly act of Jesus in an eminent degree and in a manner which is exclusively proper to her, that she could be called *Virgo sacerdos*, Virgin Priest. The analogy is profound and is all for the glory of the Blessed Virgin.

No doubt she is neither by sex nor by tribe of origin among the children of Levi. She did not receive the character and the powers which Holy Orders confer on the priests of the new Law either. And nevertheless what priest was associated with the priesthood of Christ as Mary was, by virtue of her maternity? The priest is a minister of Christ; Mary is His Mother. When she offers her Son, she does it with rights superior to those of the priest, although of another nature. She also offers Him with dispositions and acts of an incomparable comprehension and dignity. If, as we said, an angel can, in some respects, bow before a priest, every priest must bow before the Mother of God. By reason of this divine maternity, says St. Thomas, her dignity touches the infinite: *dignitatem quasi infinitam...* All the acts which she accomplishes in the function of her maternity, including those which associate her with the priesthood of Christ, thus have a dignity which exceeds our measures, because they border on the infinite. Moreover, if Scripture compares priests to gold and pure silver free from all dross, does it not also affirm "that gold is only a little sand and silver is only mud, before the divine Wisdom of which Mary is the throne." "All gold in comparison of her, is as a little sand, and silver in respect to her shall be counted as clay" [Wis. 6:9].

O you priestly souls of gold and silver, whom the grandeur of the august sacrifice envelops and whom the burden of a dignity that is fearsome to the angels themselves weighs down, be completely priests of Mary and united with Her in your priestly functions. It is as such that St. Louis-Marie de Montfort considers you and announces you. "But who shall

be those servants, slaves, and children of Mary? They shall
be the sons of Levi, well purified by the fire of great
tribulation...who shall carry the gold of love in their
heart,...etc." [*T.D.*].

We shall doubtless say that these considerations on the
holiness of the priesthood and its connections with the Mother
of God are suitable for all times. Why then dwell on it about
the end times? Will not the sacrifice of the Mass be carried
out in particular conditions of necessity and effectiveness?
How can we doubt it, when we reflect on the events of these
coming times? If, then, Mary's power, according to the
expression of Montfort, must particularly be manifested over
all the devils, it will be certainly by the virtue of the cross which
triumphed over hell, by the merits of the sacrifice of Jesus, of
which the sacrifice of our altars is only the continuation and
the application. What else does this torrent of love and mercy
of which the Saint speaks signify, and which will make the
Jews, Mohammedans and idolaters be converted, if not a
prodigious outpouring of graces, fruits of the holy Mass,
streaming through Mary's hands upon the world?

We explain consequently why during these supreme
fights satan will direct his efforts specially against the sacrifice
of the Mass. The prophet Daniel announced that the
Antichrist, of whom Antiochus was the figure, would prevail
against the perpetual sacrifice and would make it cease (Dan.
8:2, 12).

When the divine mysteries will become more rare in the
world, the faith will be obscured: *prosternetur veritas in terra*;
satan will exercise more freely his violence and deceptive
seductions with the aim of a definitive triumph...: *et faciet et
prosperabitur.*

It is about prophecy, and it is also about history. Did
not Protestantism, which opens the end times and carries in
germ all godlessness, attack especially the Eucharistic
sacrifice by dogmatic negation and the destructions of the

wars of religion? The same purpose and the same tactics were in the Revolution, which massacred or exiled priests, closed churches and tried to abolish worship. And at what do the laws of the masonic republics aim? Despoliation of churches, their secularization and the intrusion of civil power, obstacles to priestly recruitment by the abolition of ecclesiastical exemptions: nothing is spared in order to rarefy and finally cause the perpetual sacrifice to cease. If the current war is indeed exactly characterized by these words: *religio depopulata*, it is especially because the priests, torn away from their parishes, often little respected, are prevented from celebrating and exercising their ministry near the faithful, who remain deprived of them, at the risk of forgetting their duties.

Therefore, how right was Montfort to want the future apostles to be priests of Mary in order to protect the dignity of their priesthood and increase the efficacy of their ministry! When the prophet Daniel says that the enemy of God will have strength "against the continual sacrifice, because of sins" which will abound here on earth: *Robur autem datum est ei contra juge sacrificium propter peccata* [Dan. 8:12], we undoubtedly think of the sins of the faithful, but also those of tepid, lax or unworthy priests. On the other hand, what strength for the Church in these days of trial, what graces for souls, if in their holy functions the priests of Mary compensate for their powerlessness or for their imperfect dispositions by their union with Her! Promised by God in the earthly paradise, bequeathed by Jesus to all the faithful in the person of St. John, but (we cannot doubt) especially to priests, contemplated, finally, in the Apocalypse, this Woman will be in the Eucharistic sacrifice what she is everywhere: grace added to grace: "A holy woman is grace upon grace" [Eccli. 26:19]. That is to say that to the infinite power of the divine sacrifice will be added the intercession and ministry of Mary so approved by the Lord. It will also influence – and how efficaciously! – this collaboration of Mary in the other functions of the priest, which all refer to the holy Sacrifice by applying the power of it. As one who sacrifices, the priest is also a minister of the sacraments, a preacher, a mediator and a pastor. Let him be in everything a priest of Mary, acting in dependence on her, in union with Her and for her glory, if he wants "to know the mercies with which she is filled."

Chapter VI

Priests of Fire

"Who shall be those servants, slaves, and children of Mary? They shall be a burning fire of the ministers of the Lord, who shall kindle the fire of divine love everywhere..." [*T.D.*].

"Send this spirit all afire on the earth to create priests all afire there, by whose ministry may the face of the earth be renewed and Your Church reformed" [Fiery Prayer]. This request of St. Louis-Marie de Montfort follows upon words so grave and so mysterious which call and announce a reign of divine love. "When will this torrent of fire of pure love come which You must ignite over the whole earth in a manner so sweet and so violent that all nations, Turks, idolaters, and even Jews will burn with it and will be converted? *Nec est qui se abscondat a calore eius.*"

This vision of the future which the Saint describes for us, initiated in the revelations of Paray-le-Monial, is for us a vision of the present. We see, indeed, and not without admiration, the development of the devotion to the Sacred Heart, the symbol and the center of divine love. As it progressed, in spite of all the obstacles and the efforts of satan, since the days when Montfort wrote his ardent hymns, in which the doctrine and the pious practices to the Sacred Heart are condensed as in a *Summa*.

In the breath of the divine Spirit, whether it is a breeze or tempest, the fire of love was propagated with which Jesus desires so much to enkindle the world: "And what will I, but that it be kindled?" [Lk. 12:49].

In this poor world already growing cold, God wanted to warm souls, to revive in them the flame of His love by imprinting the wounds of His Passion on St. Francis's body. Then, since the growing cold was threatening to win the heart,

God saw fit to reveal to the world in a greater light the flames of His own Heart. It is the will of Jesus that they spread in the world; and how could anyone not see that the hour has come when the torrent of fire about which Montfort speaks is more than begun, since it makes astonishing progress? Theology and liturgy, devotion and the way of spirituality, the cult of the divine love with its practices of consecration, praise, union, reparation and immolation; demonstrations and associations of every order, private or social, in the family and religious or civil communities, in nations, and beyond them for the whole human race (as Leo XIII did): are these not indications there of a universal enkindling which, according to the Saint, is a sign of end times? "Let the divine fire which Jesus Christ came to bring on the earth be kindled before You kindle that of Your anger, which will reduce the whole earth to ashes" (*Prayer of the Saint*). This fire is not yet at its maximum of intensity. We await the miracles of grace and conversions announced by Montfort which have to renew the face of the earth. Shall we wait for a long time still? God alone knows the day and the hour which He fixed in His eternal Wisdom. Our attention, however, is drawn to present events, and our reflections are stimulated by the truly extraordinary concurrence of circumstances in which they are being accomplished. Why does every phase of the current crisis open new perspectives by revealing little by little a divine plan with a significance which escapes us? Would this reunion of almost all nations of the earth on the soil of France be made in view of a sort of Pentecost, so that they may be witnesses of divine prodigies? Will not the prayers so multiplied and so ardent for the reign of Christ, prayers which the Holy Spirit inspires, be granted with this superabundance which is customary of the divine mercy?

Will they be exempt from the ardors of this fire which nobody is to escape? – "there is no one that can hide himself from his heat" [Ps. 18:7] – these friends of Christ that He has made sharers of His priesthood? That is impossible, because the priesthood is not separated from love. Therefore, they are souls of fire, because they are souls of priests, and especially priests of Mary; that is what it is advisable to meditate on.

Jesus established priests as ministers of His sacrifice. It is their principal function, the others are connected with it as to their principle, and ensue from it as from their source. The graces which they distribute are the fruit of the divine Sacrifice, the center of religion, and source of the Christian life. Now this Sacrifice proceeds from love, is the supreme pledge of it, and the end through Communion in which it is consummated.

It is, indeed, in the heart God, in this sanctuary of love, that the immolation of Jesus originated. The Church chants in the Paschal hymn: *Amor sacerdos immolat.* Love becomes a priest and he immolates the sacred victim that is the body of Jesus. The apostles bore witness to it many times. St. Paul said, indeed: "Who by the Holy Ghost offered Himself unspotted unto God" [Heb. 9:14]. It is by the movement of the Spirit (Who is the love of the Father and the Son) that Jesus offered Himself to God as a spotless victim.

If it proceeds from love, the divine sacrifice is also the testimony of it to an unsurpassable degree. "Greater love than this no man hath, that a man lay down his life for his friends" [Jn. 15:13]. And what is the end of this divine immolation? It is love, because grace and salvation do not go without charity; it is union to which it leads as to its end. That is why the sacrifice is consummated in holy Communion whose direct and principal fruit is to increase, arouse, and perfect charity.

Who can read the narrative of the institution of the Eucharist and the moving conversations with which the Gospel surrounds it without feeling the love which bursts from every word, as soon as we press it by meditating on it? The Sacred Heart, so widely opened for everyone and at any hour, had never poured itself out as at these blessed moments when, anticipating the immolation of the next day, Jesus gave Himself in Communion and instituted the Christian priesthood which would perpetuate His sacrifice. At the head of the narrative of the Last Supper, St. John had put these words which reveal the pervasive theme of it: "Having loved His own who were in the world, He loved them unto the end" [Jn. 13:1]. Everything comes from the heart of God, and it is His love which is going to immolate it at the Eucharistic supper and on the cross. To close this narrative the Evangelist wrote the priestly prayer of Christ which shows Him to us asking the Father for this *unto the end*, this supreme expression of love. Jesus immolates Himself, He Who is the Priest and Victim, Pontiff and Lamb of God. By virtue of His sacrifice He will unite all those who will receive Him in Communion by the sacrament, by faith and charity. He will make them like Himself in such a way that they will become one among themselves and with Him, as He and the Father are one. "I in them, and Thou in Me; that they may be made perfect in one" [Jn. 17:23]. So it is that, as supreme High Priest, He will offer Himself to His Father with us, the members of His mystical body; and this oblation begun in the Cenacle will be perpetuated on our altars and will remain forever in glory where the union will be consummated. It will be the Mass of Heaven by Jesus, the eternal Priest. Here, then, is this *unto the end*, this end of the Incarnation, the Redemption and the whole mystery of Christ; but, as the last words of this prayer recall again, the mystery conceived by eternal love, realized by love and consuming themselves in Him: "that the love wherewith Thou hast loved Me, may be in them, and I in them" [Jn. 17:26].

How, then, can anyone participate in the priesthood of Christ without sharing in His love? What a terrifying prodigy, what an unparalleled disorder is that of the loveless or lukewarm priest who, in the very act of the sacrifice, *infra actionem*, only becomes one with Christ to the point of saying: "This is my body…This is my blood." In the face of this truly monstrous contradiction, one's thoughts abruptly and painfully turn back to the words of Jesus: "That which thou dost, do quickly" [Jn. 13:27]. Words said to the traitor, and which the Lord seems to repeat to the unworthy or tepid priest whom He hastens to remove, because he revolts His heart.

Priest of fire! The right word, which is divinely inspired, because, speaking about angels, Scripture says that God makes them ministers similar to a burning fire [Ps. 103:4]. But these pure spirits, ministers of His intentions, are not the ministers of His sacrifice. This honor and power belong to the priest who, more than they, must be a blazing fire. The fact that fire always tends to rise, that it is quick and subtle, are the properties which commentators attributed to the ministers of the Lord, angels or priests. Note, however, the idea on which the sacred text insists: *ignem urentem*, a burning fire, because it comes out of the heart of the same God Who is a consuming fire, "Because the Lord thy God is a consuming fire" [Dt. 4:24]. This fire of love with which these apostles will be filled, they will spread through the world to consume the iniquities in it, to purify it of stains and transform it in charity. Then they will need it especially in these times when, according to the divine Master Himself, the abundance of the iniquities will make charity grow cold in a large number of hearts [cf. Mt. 24:12]!

But who will bring us close to this furnace of love that is the heart of Jesus, a furnace burning to excess when the Passion came, "and the furnace was heated exceedingly" [Dan. 3:22]? Who will make it possible for us to throw ourselves in it without our weakness and stains making us dread the consuming and purifying heat of its flames, *they were sent into the furnace not fearing the flame of the fire*? Finally, who will teach us to praise and bless God there: *saying: blessed be God?* The Gospel gives us the response. Jesus gives the name of "friends" to all His apostles; all are ordained priests, all have tasted (in what delightful contemplation!) the conversations of the divine Master. Only one, however, at these solemn moments had with Him a very enviable familiarity; it was St. John, the beloved of Jesus, and of Mary whose priest he would be. She, through whom every grace comes to us, obtained for John the unique privilege of resting on the heart of Jesus at the time of his priestly ordination. He got close to this burning hearth more than the others and cast himself into it. In this closeness, what did he know of the love from which the redeeming sacrifice proceeds; with what ardors was he inflamed by listening to the beating of the Sacred Heart? To complete his priestly education, Mary led him, still alone among the apostles, to the sacrifice of the cross; and there, as at the Last Supper, Mary's priest was the friend *par excellence*, the close friend of the Sacred Heart, the assistant of the divine Victim, the favorite of His love. In his person all the faithful, but especially priests, were given to Mary and received her into their homes as their mother. In his person also, after resting on the divine Heart, they obtained the grace to see Him half-opened and pierced, to peer attentively into the interior of this sanctuary: "They shall look on him whom they pierced" [Jn. 19:37]. It is because, according to the beautiful remark of St. Louis-Marie de Montfort, Mary alone received from God the keys of the storerooms of divine love, and the power to enter the most sublime and most secret ways of perfection and to admit others there.

St. Louis-Marie de Montfort was, like St. John, a favorite of Mary, her priest and her apostle, who was also a priest of fire and an ardent friend of the Sacred Heart. Nowhere shall we find more fiery accents, more urgent zeal, feelings of more delightful intimacy than in his writings, and in particular in his hymns about the Passion, the Eucharist and the Sacred Heart. If the expression: "ministers a burning fire" [Ps. 103:4] suits any mortal sent by the Lord, it assuredly suits this priest of fire who preached, even more than he wrote, his *Fiery Prayer* whose accents, after more than two centuries, still warm souls.

These are very attractive considerations for those who have the responsibility to form and sanctify priests. Let them be, then, priests of Mary; she will make them priests of fire. The disciples in Emmaus, hesitating, diminished in zeal, and almost discouraged, felt their heart being enkindled again by listening to Jesus, Who walked with them and explained the Scriptures to them. "Was not our heart burning within us, whilst He spoke in this way, and opened to us the Scriptures"

[Lk. 24:32]? What will happen to those whom Jesus no longer calls servants, but "friends," because, He says, "all things whatsoever I have heard of My Father, I have made known to you" [Jn. 15:15]. Let Mary prepare them for the secrets of the Lord! For priests, they are a daily occurrence and of such a high caliber! Priestly secrets, in which Jesus would like to say so much to us and to communicate with us! But, alas! He often has to hold back and keep silent, because we are unworthy and incapable! Let this Mother and Mistress dilate, then, our souls and dispose them for the effusions of the Spirit of love! Jesus immolated Himself by the movement of this divine Spirit; and we, in priestly functions, are moved only by Him. Let us pray with Montfort so that these priests of fire will come who will renew the face of the earth.

Chapter VII

Priest and Victim

In Jesus, let us not separate what God has joined: He is at the same time Priest and victim, the One Who offers sacrifice and the victim; He is named the Lamb of God. This is why Mary, who follows the Lamb wherever He goes, in His ways of humiliation or glory, who participates in all His mysteries and faithfully associates herself with His conditions, Mary offers Him to God and offers herself in union with Him. In the temple, as on Calvary, we have no difficulty in perceiving these two acts, so clearly do they appear in the narrative of the Gospel.

On the day of His Presentation in the Temple, Jesus offered Himself by the hands of His Mother; and this oblation which she made in virtue of the rights of her divine maternity associated her in a special and eminent way to the act of Jesus the High Priest. But at the same time she was united to His state of victim. She offered herself to be immolated, and already Simeon's words thrust into her soul the two-edged sword which would end by piercing it. When the Passion of her Son would come later, the Blessed Virgin would be associated with it by her compassion to a degree so excellent that she would deserve the title of Co-redemptrix. But the Passion of Jesus and the Compassion of Mary form one mystery; they were the simultaneous offering and immolation of the hearts of the Son and the Mother, inseparable in the divine decrees. When the Heart of Jesus was opened by the lance, His soul had left His body; but that of Mary could not be torn from the foot of the Cross; it was pierced through there, and so was her immolation consummated: with Jesus, Mary was a victim.

The Virgin desires to imbue her children with this spirit of sacrifice and this role of victim, especially her favorites. Does not her first consecrated one, John the Baptist, whom she went to sanctify and form during her stay with Elizabeth,

John the Baptist, the future precursor, distinguish himself by a life of self-sacrifice to a very high degree? He preaches penance, and from his childhood he sets an example of it by the austerity of his life: *Vinum et siceram non bibet.* His clothing, his food, and his stay in the desert command our attention. But (even more remarkable!) this favorite son of Mary, enlightened by a bright light, recognized in the Messiah the quality of a victim and pointed Him out to the crowds in these words: "Behold the Lamb of God, behold Him Who taketh away the sin of the world [Jn. 1:29]: *Ecce Agnus Dei.*"

To her priests who, in the exercise of their priesthood, want to be imbued with its spirit, Mary inculcates, then, the thought and the desire to be at the same time priests and victims in order to be conformed to Jesus. In this we can also observe that the hearts of Jesus and Mary became one; that this Virgin is an excellent Teacher to teach the ways of God; and that to follow her is to follow Jesus faithfully. The divine Master, indeed, did not proceed otherwise in the formation of His apostles, and in particular St. John. On Tabor He made him a witness of this momentary manifestation of His glory, during which He spoke of His death, His excess of love. "And they spoke of His decease" [Lk. 9:31]. We cannot doubt that in the Cenacle, the beloved disciple was also occupied with the Passion, when he rested on this divine Heart, which was already wounded by treason, and whose beatings of ardent charity he heard: "With desire I have desired to eat this Pasch with you, before I suffer" [Lk. 22:15]. The teaching of the Master and the secrets of the divine Friend were still advancing. Better still than on glorious Tabor, John had then an understanding of the sacrifice and of the language of Jesus speaking about His body which would be handed over, about His blood which would be poured out. And it was infinite love which urged Jesus to immolate Himself by also enkindling this beloved one and drawing him to the Cross. He went there, this faithful Apostle, by following Mary. She had to teach him his office of victim, to give him the understanding and the sense of these words: "With Christ I am nailed to the cross. And I live, now not I; but Christ liveth in me" [Gal. 2:19-20].

This love of the cross commands the attention of whoever reads the life of St. Louis-Marie de Montfort, and his biographers in every age emphatically pointed it out. Other saints undoubtedly distinguished themselves by a passionate desire for sacrifice; but what characterizes Montfort, is that he learned this science at the school of Mary. Just as St. John did, it is in following the Most Blessed Virgin that he ascended to Calvary. Assiduous in the school of this divine Mistress, the apostles of the end times will draw with a burning love the desire to be victims in order to sacrifice themselves with Jesus. It is about them, indeed, that Montfort speaks in these terms: "By their abandonment to Providence and their devotion to Mary, they will have the silvery wings of the dove and a golden back, that is to say, a perfect love of neighbor... and a great love for Jesus Christ to carry His Cross. (Prayer) – Further on, commenting on the text of the Psalm: "a curdled mountain, a fat mountain" [Ps. 67:16], he adds: "It is on this mountain of God (which is Mary)... that they will die with Him as on Calvary." And in the pages of the *True Devotion*, very often quoted, he represents to us these future apostles, children and slaves of Mary, carrying the gold of love in their heart, the incense of prayer in their spirit, and the myrrh of mortification in their heart. They have the crucifix in their right hand and the Rosary in their left.

The life as the writings of the Saint show him to us very advanced in the science of the Cross; a science superior and sublime that he learned at the maternal school of Mary through the dealings of a mother with a little child; because, he says, Mary sweetens the hardest crosses for us by steeping them in the sugar of her sweetness.

Did we, indeed, notice enough in these apostles imbued with the spirit of the Cross and formed by Mary, the double character of strength and sweetness by which they resemble their Mother? They are sweet, because she is a woman; but they are strong, because she is the strong Woman. Contemplate them all, these Sons of the Virgin whom she forms in her image and whom she arms against the enemies of God; Elias, John the Baptist, St. Louis-Marie de Montfort. In them austerity of life, courage in battle, sacrifice till death become allied with the tenderness and the indulgences of divine charity for little ones, the poor, sinners, and souls of good will.

We shall doubtless say that the love of the Cross is a fundamental and indispensable thing in the Christian life; that any priest would be disordered in his priestly life if he did not become a victim and partake of the Passion of Jesus. Why then do we emphasize this necessity of immolation in the apostles of the end times? Will there be for these priests a more urgent need to have compassion with Christ, both for their own sanctification and because of their apostolate? We could not doubt it.

If in these times, which will have had no equal, evil is to grow in extent, power, and boldness, it is necessary for holiness also to rise up in proportion to it, and surpass it in order to triumph over it. If, then, the pride of those who hate God will keep increasing, "the pride of them that hate Thee ascendeth continually" [Ps. 73:23], on the other hand Montfort asserts that then Mary will form great saints who will surpass in holiness most of the other saints [cf. *T.D.*]. Is there a need to investigate how? He himself tells us that these children of Levi, these priests, will be purified by the fire of great tribulations. Tribulations and sufferings from the outside or the inside, as he himself had so much to bear, which will expand their souls in God, according to the word of the Psalmist: "In distress Thou hast enlarged me" [Ps. 4:2]. A regime of strength, formation in courage, as the habitual communion with the Passion of the Christ. These future apostles, says Montfort, will have the strength of an ox by their mortifications. They will be brave and strong.

But someone who joins himself to the immolation of Jesus enters, according to the original and profound expression of Scripture, into the power of the Lord. There is the secret of the prodigious efficacy which the apostolate of these great servants of God will have; because they will preach like the Apostles, *virtute magna*. It is by His cross that the Savior conquered satan; and when He will come to judge the world, it will be His glorious standard which will rally all the faithful, no longer for battle, but for triumph; the cross will be, therefore, the weapon of these fighters and a rod to work miracles greater than those of Aaron's rod.

Here are the apostles whom satan dreads and whom he tries hard to weaken in order to enfeeble their apostolate. He uses everything to this end: the infiltration of bad doctrines, pride, laxity, dissipation, and the love of ease, which quickly spoil priestly holiness. He works on it by the diffusion of ideas called modern, by the laws of an atheistic State, by the habits of life in certain circles. His purpose is to secularize the priesthood by breathing into it the spirit of the world, and to decrease this fullness of religion that the Council of Trent demands for the cleric in all his acts, *religione plenum*.

It is a painful necessity that priests be, in the first place, victims for the priesthood. There are under this heading some reparations and indisputable expiations. But priests also have to sanctify themselves in the degree that the extreme dangers and the needs of the times which we pass through require; and it is very satisfying to see them becoming priests of Mary. Is it not near Her that the apostles, even unfaithful, gathered in their repentant love? The intercession of the Mother of mercy merited for them the grace of hearing, from the first meeting with the risen Jesus, this greeting: "Peace be with you" [Jn. 20:19]. Near Mary, if he had come to her, Judas might have done expiation and reparation.

But the great office of mediator and Victim, which, like Jesus, priests have to perform, becomes more necessary as the reign of sin extends. For a long time the liturgy of Lent has sung this response: *Inter vestibulum et altare plorabunt sacerdotes et ministri Domini*. Holier, more pleasing to God in order to draw down His mercy than the part of the Temple designated above is Mary, our divine oratory, as Montfort calls her. In all truth, we can apply these words to her: *Locus iste sanctus est in quo orat sacerdos pro delictis et peccatis populi.* Jesus, our eternal High Priest, prayed there from His Incarnation; and it is in union with the immaculate Heart of His Mother that He always implored His heavenly Father.

The ideas and habits which we dread to see prevailing in the priestly life, and which favor dreadful living conditions imposed on priests since the war, inspire in the Church a just solicitude for the future of the priesthood. Are not these views of St. Louis-Marie de Montfort a very opportune sign? Will not the priests who will enjoy them and conform their life to them justify all expectations and holy ambitions? They will not only return, as so many people ardently desire it (thanks be to God!), to their normal environment; they will not only be invigorated in the spirit of their holy state; but they, whom the war so suddenly confronted with abnormal situations, will also be found, on their return, in the presence of a restoration of society in Christ and an immense apostolate in every direction. Near Mary they will be inspired by the true spirit which must animate their apostolate and will draw from it the strength to undertake it successfully. It is she, indeed, who will make shine the grace of their priesthood, and will make of them priests of fire and victims immolated with Jesus for the salvation of the world.

"Happy and a thousand times happy are the priests whom you chose so well and predestined to live with you on this plentiful and divine mountain (which is Mary), to become kings of eternity by their contempt of the earth and their devotion to God; so as to become whiter there than snow by their union with Mary, your all-beautiful Spouse, all pure and all immaculate; so as to grow rich with the dew of Heaven and the fat of the land, with all the temporal and eternal blessings with which Mary is completely filled." (*Prayer.*)

Chapter VIII

The Apostolate of the End Times

When we read what St. Louis-Marie de Montfort wrote about this subject, we have the feeling of a renewed Pentecost. Not surprising since the two ages will correspond with each other by an asymmetrical likeness, so to speak; *a dissimilar likeness*, the ancients used to say. Pentecost opens the course of the Church, whose last times prepare for the closure; but in both cases, it is still Christian evangelization. The first time, Christ was preached to a world in which He came and which did not know Him; the second time, His return will be announced to this world which denied Him. At Pentecost, it was necessary to Christianize; now it is a matter of restoring all things in Christ: *omnia restaurare in Christo*. At Pentecost, the apostolic preaching followed the victory of the Lord over death and hell; but, at the end of time, it will prepare for His triumphal return and His definitive victory. Such is the similarity of the apostolic ministry in the two ages. It is possible, however, that in the second it will require more power and that the battle may be more fierce. In this world, indeed, which was already delivered from the yoke of satan, the enemy has returned to despoil it of its true goods; and, as the Gospel says, its last state is worse than the first: *et erunt novissima eius peiora prioribus* [Mt. 12:45]. Anyone who shall have rejected grace will return to God with more difficulty. On the other hand, hell, conscious of its upcoming defeat and consummation, will fight desperately. We conceive, therefore, that the combat then will be more violent, that the antagonism of the two races will be more clear-cut and – which we can now glimpse – that the parties of the happy medium will be obliterated in the face of extremes. Yes or no, God or satan, Christ or Antichrist, the Church or Freemasonry, the synagogue of satan: these are the opposites between which it will be necessary to choose.

We are speaking of a new Pentecost, because then, as previously, there will be an occurrence, an extraordinary influx of the Holy Spirit, and the similarity in the circumstances and way will not be absent. Here are, indeed, the words of the Saint that we have already quoted and which are very explicit: "Then will end the reign of the Spirit of the Father and of the Son by a deluge of fire and pure love... Send this Spirit all aflame on the earth to renew and reform Your Church... The Holy Spirit came at Pentecost under the form of tongues of fire; He will come again also on these future apostles, whom He will enkindle and who will preach by His power." These imitators of the apostles, these priests all afire, says Montfort, will preach *with great power*. Without speaking of the prodigies which will support their words, we cannot doubt the marvelous effects that it will work, as did that of the Apostles at Pentecost. "They will preach with great strength and virtue; and so great, and so resounding, that they will move all minds and hearts in the places where they preach − It is to them that You will give Your word which none of their enemies will be able to resist. "I will give you a mouth and wisdom, which all your adversaries shall not be able to resist" [Lk. 21:15].

These thoughts explain the devotion that the Saint professed to the Holy Spirit, of Whom Mary is the dear and inseparable Spouse. "It is with her, in her, and of her, that He had produced His Masterpiece, which is a God made Man, and whom He goes on producing in the persons of His members daily to the end of the world. The predestinate are the members of that adorable Head" [*T.D.*]. Montfort, then, could not give himself so perfectly to Mary without having a special devotion to the divine Spirit. But, besides this general consideration, there are several special ones which are connected with his prophetic views. This new Pentecost, this deluge of a fire of love, and these prodigies of the apostolate will be the work of the Holy Spirit. How necessary it will be to invoke Him, to surrender to His action, and not even to grieve Him: "And grieve not the holy Spirit of God" [Eph. 4:30]. From where will come to these inflamed priests the power which may cause them to renew the face of the earth? From this Spirit Who formerly filled the heart of Stephen and gave to his word a force which his hearers could not resist: "Stephen...full of faith and of the Holy Ghost" [Acts 6:5]. But, it is also by Him that the Antichrist will be conquered. Jesus will dissipate the fantasy of his usurped kingdom and apparent victories and kill this man of sin with a breath of His mouth: "whom the Lord Jesus shall kill with the spirit of His mouth" [2 Th. 2:8].

Then, in view of these end times, Montfort could not separate the Holy Spirit from Mary, the Bridegroom from the Bride, because what is done by this divine Spirit is done through Mary. In the Cenacle, after the prayer of Jesus in glory, that of Mary took precedence over all others and hastened the coming of the Holy Spirit. He rested, first of all, on Her and from there spread over the Apostles. The mystery will continue in the Pentecost of the end times. This effusion of the Holy Spirit will happen at the intercession of Mary, and it is through Her that He will come upon the new apostles who will be particularly devoted to her.

There is no need to reflect for a long time in order to understand that the apostolate of these ardent missionaries will be clearly Marian. Such will be its characteristic. Mary must prepare the second coming of Jesus, as she prepared the first. It is the application to this particular event of the teaching that St. Louis-Marie de Montfort teaches: "Mary is the way by which Jesus comes to us, and it is by Her that we go to Jesus" [cf. *T.D.*]: but this novel and original application provokes interesting reflections.

These apostles will preach Mary: because the time will exist no longer (it is no longer already), in which Jansenism tried to veil the splendor of this masterpiece of God. St. John sees her clothed with the sun; and far from obscuring the glory of God, this Woman shines with it. Like a spotless mirror, she reflects it on the world. To make her known will be, then, to glorify the Lord, and to propagate her cult will be at the same time to promote that which is rendered to God and to His Son Jesus.

This coming of Christ in souls by grace, and finally in person on this earth for the general judgment, is the object of the prayers and sighs of holy souls. Mary will be at their head; and, as formerly for the Incarnation or for the descent of the Holy Spirit at Pentecost, this all-powerful suppliant – *omnipotentia supplex,* – this spouse, beloved among all, the unique one of the Lord, will be listened to with kindness. The Church will pray in union with Her; but to those who are specially dedicated to her, to her consecrated ones and to her priests, will not Mary give a special share in the unspeakable groans of the divine Spirit... *Spiritus postulat gemitibus inenarrabilibus*? The answer is already given by the facts. Let us recall how St. John, the beloved son of Mary, longed for the coming of Jesus. He finished the visions of his Apocalypse with these appeals. And is this prayer of St. Louis-Marie de Montfort, who asks to die rather than not be answered, anything other than an ardent longing? By giving to her own this Spirit of grace and prayer, Mary prepares for the second coming of Jesus.

But Jesus told us: He will come as a thief, and the parable of the virgins is always present in our mind. What help, then, will this Virgin most prudent be, *Virgo prudentissima*, to keep souls vigilant and to dispose them for this coming, sooner or later, of Christ? Especially since the seductions are also predicted. False prophets, false Christs or Messiahs will appear. But for all, especially for those who belong to her totally, Mary is the safe, sure, straight, and immaculate way to go to Jesus Christ and to find Him perfectly; it is by her that the saints who have to shine in holiness must find Him [cf. *T.D.*].

Finally, in these last times, Mary has to make her power over all the demons shine more than ever. Montfort insists on this point, not without a great accuracy of views. More than ever, indeed, we shall have to fight less against the forces of flesh and blood, against a human power, than against the spiritual forces or the powers of darkness [cf. Eph. 6:12]. The action of the evil spirits will show itself more. They are the ones who lead the fight against the Church with a skill and a stubborn hatred of which man alone is not capable. To this kind of diabolical possession, or, if we want, to this servitude of the henchmen of satan, will be opposed the holy slavery of Mary or the total belonging of her devotees. The role of the Virgin therein appears, then, clearly with the means of apostolate and the battle which will be suited to the circumstances.

The holy Archangel Michael is the generalissimo of this army of the Virgin in the orders of his Queen. At the head of the faithful angels, he led the fight against Lucifer; he continues it with the Church militant according to the ways of divine Wisdom, where everything is coherent and coordinated up to the end. From now on he assists this Church and has the mandate to offer the prayers of the saints, to lead souls into paradise, and come to the aid of the people of God. And when the end times will come, which will have no equal since the world began to exist, the glorious Archangel will rise, and standing up, in the attitude of combat and command, will assure the salvation of the children of the chosen people. "But at that time shall Michael rise up, the great prince, who standeth for the children of thy people" [Dan 12:1]. Thus is explained the devotion of St. Louis-Marie de Montfort to St. Michael. It was in order to commend to him his own battles, as well as those of his future missionaries, that he made a pilgrimage to his famous shrine in Normandy; and in order to draw us one after another to this head and model, he makes this appeal: "Like no one else will St. Michael exclaim in the midst of his brothers while striving zealously for Your glory: *Quis ut Deus*?" (*Prayer.*)

The prayer of St. Louis-Marie de Montfort is, in the first place, for his dear Company of Mary, which must continue his missions. This is what he asks of God in explicit terms, with an ardent faith and a love which inspires in him deeds of holy audacity. He urges, however, all good priests to join with him in order to fight under the standard of Mary. This wish of the holy missionary was realized by the Association of Priests of

Mary, and it is to them also that these pages are addressed. In the same vein, Fr. Faber wrote: "I return insistently to this prayer *all those* who have difficulty in preserving, in the midst of their numerous trials, the first fires of love for souls." What a holy and sweet thing, even in memory alone, are these first fires of love for souls! How much we wish to see them enkindled and how we worry to feel them weakening or going out! So many causes contribute to it: crises of the interior life, the inadequacy of one's union with Jesus, which makes the soul cast itself outside, become external and arid; finally, failures and disappointments, pressure and very diverse temptations. Is it not together with Mary that, in the first years of his priesthood, the priest can constantly revive the flame of his zeal, avoid or overcome dangers? By faithfully following this immaculate way, which is Mary, he will reconcile his youth with his rank of priest (*presbyter*, elder), and in him will be justified then this sentence of Scripture: "And a spotless life is old age" [Wis. 4:9].

Years will pass by, and experience has shown that we could interpret the noonday devil (*a daemonio meridiano*) to be this environment of life where, as a result of the infirmity of our nature, weariness and disappointments, we tend to withdraw into ourselves, to descend to the joys or the consolations of earth. *Ut mentes nostras ad caelestia desideria erigas!* It is the duty of a mother supporting her child, who always tends to bow towards the ground. He would inevitably fall down without the help of a maternal hand, which lifts him up at every moment. How could we fail to remember here the assurances which Montfort loves to repeat and which we shall find near "Her who keeps the saints in their plenitude and makes them persevere till the end? And the *Speculum B.V.*, attributed to St. Bonaventure, so details the meaning of this word: "Mary prevents virtues from disappearing, merits from being lost, graces from being squandered, and the demons from harming us."

And as we are facing the end times, their ordeals, their fights, their characteristic apostolate, which will require a special caliber of soul, an indefatigable courage, is it not the strong Woman battling against the dragon who will sustain the courage of her children and apostles? The present generation, which is heading towards its end and of whom many have left this world, is living through terrible days at this moment. We can affirm, however, that they are less distressing than those which have elapsed for approximately half a century. The fight against God became more marked and widespread; nothing stopped the progress of evil and error; destructions succeeded destructions; the Church, in her Head as in her members, was persecuted; the boldness of those who hate God rose more and more, and their power seemed to become stronger. "How long, O Lord: *Usquequo, Domine*?" moaned the faithful souls. But God seemed to sleep. Behold how the storm suddenly bursts out, violent, disastrous, and universal; but we are afforded a glimpse of the outcome.

The triumph and the restoration are approaching: the mourning and sacrifices assure it and hasten their coming. These days and these fears of the hours which God grants to the power of darkness will doubtless return, darker and graver still. In order to remain, like St. John, strong in their love and faith, these apostles of the end times will have only to remain near the Woman whose love and faith in the Resurrection, even after Calvary and the tomb, did not weaken for a single instant. While grappling with the powers of hell, and whatever may be its apparent triumphs, their faith will remain unalterable and will assure them the victory. "And this is the victory which overcometh the world, our faith" [1 Jn. 5:4]. Lord Jesus, remember to give to your Mother a new Company, to renew everything by Her, and to finish through Mary the years of grace, as you began them through Her [St. Louis-Marie de Montfort].

AMEN

GOD ALONE

45061930R00043

Made in the USA
Middletown, DE
23 June 2017